"This compact, helpfully structured book contains a wealth of information about the range of couple therapies available to those seeking help. The author brings her considerable knowledge and experience to provide valuable insights into the rationale behind different approaches and illustrates how these are put into practice. The result is an accessible and intriguing resource that will be of real value to couples seeking help, to practitioners making referrals, and to those considering training to be a couple therapist."

Christopher Clulow, *PhD, consultant couple psychotherapist and senior fellow of the Tavistock Institute of Medical Psychology*

"Clear, succinct and attractive in format, *Couple Therapy: The Basics* by a leader in the field, Molly Ludlam, provides an excellent resource for beginning therapists and supervisors alike to think psychoanalytically about couples, couple therapy and couple supervision."

Jill Savege Scharff, *MD, FABP, MRC Psych, co-author of* Object Relations Couple Therapy, *co-founder of the International Psychotherapy Institute*

"Molly Ludlam provides a comprehensive and accessible overview of the field of couple therapy, whilst also homing in on key, in depth, elements of this approach. Her style of writing is open, inclusive and reflective and will stimulate the reader's curiosity at every turn. This book will be extremely valuable to anyone who might be considering couple therapy for their relationship or as a career."

Mary Morgan, *psychoanalyst, senior fellow of Tavistock Relationships*

COUPLE THERAPY
THE BASICS

Couple Therapy: The Basics provides a comprehensive introduction to couple therapy. Taking both a general overview and a psychoanalytic focus, it addresses the basic questions that both couples and those interested in becoming couple therapists can expect to ask.

Using jargon-light language, this book summarises the range of approaches available to those seeking couple therapy – from behavioural to psychoanalytic. It covers topics such as: what defines a couple, challenges for couple therapists, and outcomes for couple therapy. While introducing the subject to many readers, it also aims to further interest in and understanding of couple therapy, explaining its differences from other therapies. A glossary of key terms is included, as well as appendices with links to research and associated organisations.

This book is essential for early career therapists, as well as those undertaking or interested in couple therapy.

Molly Ludlam, MA, is a couple and individual psychoanalytic psychotherapist and contributor to many books and journals, and was the founding editor of *Couple and Family Psychoanalysis* (2011–2019). Now retired from clinical practice, and as a course teacher and examiner, she currently focuses on consulting and writing.

The Basics Series

The Basics is a highly successful series of accessible guidebooks which provide an overview of the fundamental principles of a subject area in a jargon-free and undaunting format.

Intended for students approaching a subject for the first time, the books both introduce the essentials of a subject and provide an ideal springboard for further study. With over 50 titles spanning subjects from artificial intelligence (AI) to women's studies, *The Basics* are an ideal starting point for students seeking to understand a subject area.

Each text comes with recommendations for further study and gradually introduces the complexities and nuances within a subject.

BDSM AND KINK
Stefani Goerlich and Elyssa Helfer

SIMONE DE BEAUVOIR
Megan Burke

INTERVIEWING: THE BASICS
Mark Holton

SHAKESPEARE (FOURTH EDITION)
Sean McEvoy

For a full list of titles in this series, please visit www.routledge.com/The-Basics/book-series/B

COUPLE THERAPY

THE BASICS

Molly Ludlam

Routledge
Taylor & Francis Group

NEW YORK AND LONDON

Designed cover image: severija © Getty Images

First published 2025
by Routledge
605 Third Avenue, New York, NY 10158

and by Routledge
4 Park Square, Milton Park, Abingdon, Oxon, OX14 4RN

Routledge is an imprint of the Taylor & Francis Group, an informa business

© 2025 Molly Ludlam

Library of Congress Cataloging-in-Publication Data
Names: Ludlam, Molly, author.
Title: Couple therapy : the basics / Molly Ludlam.
Description: New York, NY : Routledge, 2024. | Series: The basics series | Includes bibliographical references and index. |
Identifiers: LCCN 2024005926 (print) | LCCN 2024005927 (ebook) | ISBN 9781032322100 (hardback) | ISBN 9781032317090 (paperback) | ISBN 9781003313403 (ebook)
Subjects: LCSH: Couples therapy.
Classification: LCC RC488.5 .L795 2024 (print) | LCC RC488.5 (ebook) | DDC 616.89/1562--dc23/eng/20240509
LC record available at https://lccn.loc.gov/2024005926
LC ebook record available at https://lccn.loc.gov/2024005927

ISBN: 978-1-032-32210-0 (hbk)
ISBN: 978-1-032-31709-0 (pbk)
ISBN: 978-1-003-31340-3 (ebk)

DOI: 10.4324/9781003313403

Typeset in Bembo
by KnowledgeWorks Global Ltd.

To our children, Naomi and Michael, and to my parents, Irene and Charles, in recognition of all that they have contributed to my understanding of couple and family relationships.

CONTENTS

ACKNOWLEDGEMENTS

I want first to acknowledge my gratitude to all the couples and families with whom I have worked and with whom I have learned so much about therapeutic relationships. I am indebted too to couple psychotherapy colleagues in the UK and internationally for the continuing opportunity to share enriching learning and for the privilege of participating with them on the *Journal of Couple and Family Psychoanalysis*. I am especially grateful to Mary Morgan for her support, to Audrey Neill for her generosity, as well as to my writing group companions, Liz Bondi and Judith Fewell. Thank you also to Sarah Rae at Routledge for her sustained and sustaining encouragement. Finally, however, this book could not have been written without the loving support of Christopher Ludlam, my keenest critic, whose tolerance and belief has accompanied me throughout this and many other journeys.

INTRODUCTION TO COUPLE THERAPY

OVERVIEW

This introductory chapter begins by stating the book's aims and the readership it hopes to interest. Together with an overview of the next twelve chapters' main themes, each of which will emphasise the importance of readers' curiosity, this chapter discusses why couple relationships matter so much. It asks what place couple therapy has in our society and considers it in five separate dimensions. It goes on to explain the book's use of composite case examples, and to explore the use of associated language, such as 'therapy', 'work', and 'diversity'. Finally, readers are left with questions inviting them to enquire further.

WHO IS THIS BOOK FOR?

Couple Therapy: The Basics is designed as a basic resource and to whet the appetite of anyone interested in expanding their critical understanding of couple therapy. You may be:

- Considering seeking couple therapy for yourself and your partner;
- Curious about whether to pursue training as a couple therapist;
- Interested because the couples you meet in your work setting (paid or voluntary) might benefit from your greater understanding;
- Teaching and supervising colleagues who are working, or planning to work, as couple therapists.

DOI: 10.4324/9781003313403-1

WHAT ARE ITS AIMS?

This book aims to offer an overview of the wide field of couple therapy. As currently practised, couple therapy is enormously varied and, sadly, in this slim volume there is not enough space to be as comprehensive or satisfactory in breadth or depth as all readers might wish. Each chapter, while referencing others, is intended also to be 'stand-alone', but because of the inherent interrelatedness of couples and couple therapy, some repetition has been inevitable. Although limited, the book nevertheless aims to inspire further inquiry, and to address the basic questions about this form of therapy which both couples and those interested in becoming couple therapists might ask.

VALUING YOUR CURIOSITY

Whatever your starting point in picking up this book up, it is hoped that your curiosity will be continually stimulated by the thinking that it aims to provoke. Each chapter includes and ends with questions which the reader is invited think further about, whether alone or in discussion with others. The book's reference lists and Bibliography are thus suggested resources for more detailed enquiry.

THE CONTEXT FOR THIS BOOK

Why is this book important now? 'Why now?' echoes a question that couple therapists repeatedly ask. All books reflect something of their author's experience while writing. The backdrop for this book has been the privations of COVID-19 and its continuing aftermath, with their evolving impacts on couple and family relationships; how we cope when locked down together or separated, with shared loss and change, or loneliness, and how well the therapies designed to support relationships can adapt to new life-changing challenges, are all part of a continuing story. From 2020, the necessity of meeting remotely, while not new, caused a revolution in the practice of talking therapies, challenging perceptions about what is necessary and desirable. Online therapy is discussed in Chapters 9 and 10.

NAVIGATING YOUR WAY THROUGH THIS BOOK

COUPLES

While this book's focus is on couple *therapy*, understanding it as a kind of therapy also involves understanding couples' relationships – what makes them work and why there may be difficulties in making them happy. The couple relationship itself, rather than the partners who make up a relationship, is therefore the starting point of the book. Chapter 2 discusses the question 'What is a couple?' and Chapter 3, the question 'Why do couples seek therapy?' In reality, if their relationship is going to be sufficiently rewarding for them to stay together, all couples need to accept that some adjustments in their relationship will be necessary to enable it to grow. For some, that adjusting feels like hard work and too much to ask; for others, the changes involved feel more like the growing pains that were part of becoming adults. Most often, couples carry out their own continual repair and restore service, their own 'everyday therapy', perhaps with the support of family and friends. Sometimes, however, couples find that they need the help of a complete outsider to support them through what would otherwise prove to be overly challenging and painful transitions.

Why Do Couple Relationships Matter So Much?

• *Couples play a key role in all human relationships.* (See also Chapter 2). They carry so many of our positive expectations, whether our desires for romance, seeking security, having a family, and/or children. But couples also embody negative expectations, such as fears of feeling disappointed, or being trapped, or the trauma of being abandoned. Family relationships are interconnected. From early childhood, expectations of adult life are influenced by growing up with siblings and our parents as a couple. Children are affected by their parents' relationship, and parental couples worry and sometimes fight over their children's wellbeing.

   Couple relationships and our ideas about them continually evolve as our lives and society change around them. How our key relationships are formed, are held onto, or break down is of constant interest and concern to human-kind the world over.

- *Committing to a lasting couple relationship is a major life decision* – one of the biggest an adult can make. And although the rate of formal agreements – whether through marriage or civil partnership – is at its lowest for over 100 years, there is a continuing, lively interest, if not preoccupation, in dating, finding a sexual partner, and the hope of coupling happily with another. It follows therefore, as many songs express, that breaking up is really heartbreaking, not only for the couple, but because the pain runs with a ripple effect through the lives of children and other family members. This leads many to ask whether couple therapy could help.

COUPLE THERAPY

'What is couple therapy?' is the focus of Chapter 4. It seems a simple question, but a closer look offers no simple answers, and has proved quite challenging to address in a summary form. Couple relationships, of course, come in all shapes and sizes. They are thus quite complex, and couple therapy, over some seventy years, has adapted several different approaches and methods to meet couples' differing needs. Couple therapies therefore also come in many forms, drawing on a wide range of theories and ways of understanding human relationships. While some aim to offer brief therapy, others are long-term and intensive.

Hence, couple therapy might be thought of as having a number of different dimensions, as outlined in Figure 1.1 and described in more detail in the sections that follow.

The Skills Dimension

Chapter 5 summarises the range of skills which a competent couple therapist would hope to bring to the work. While a number of these are also required in other forms of talking therapies, some are specific to couple therapy. The specific skills and techniques used by each approach are dictated by the theoretical basis on which it is founded.

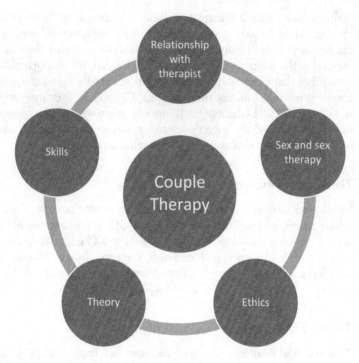

Figure 1.1 Five dimensions of couple therapy

The Theoretical Dimension

Chapter 6 gives an overview of how the different types of therapy differ and what might be expected from each. Using that broad theoretical perspective as a basis, Chapter 7 describes in greater detail, 'What is psychodynamic-psychoanalytic couple therapy?' – a perspective that reflects this author's particular interest and expertise. Further applications of this approach are set out in Chapter 8. A characteristic of this way of working is that it explores not only the relationship between the partners in a couple but also the relationship between the couple and their therapist.

The Relationship Dimension

The success of all kinds of couple therapy greatly depends on a match between what the couple is looking for and the skill and commitment of their therapist. Talking therapies work best when they are based on a trusted relationship. Although, in the course of the therapy, many intimate issues will be discussed, that does not mean that the relationship is a friendship. Indeed, it is important to remember that a therapeutic relationship essentially is and remains a *working* relationship. For these reasons, Chapter 9, 'First meetings with a couple' and Chapter 10, 'Ongoing meetings and challenges in couple therapy' are given over to exploring the nature of that relationship; what makes it work, and what hinders it.

The Sexual Dimension

Sexual satisfaction and compatibility are important in most couple relationships, and usually, but not always, they go hand-in-hand with emotional satisfaction and compatibility. The sexual dimension of couple therapy is included here, but those looking for more detailed and specific aspects of sex therapy are recommended to read Cate Campbell's *Sex Therapy: The Basics* (2023).

The Ethical Dimension

This essential dimension is thought about in Chapter 12, 'Why is supervision important for couple therapy?', emphasising a supervisor's role in helping the therapist to keep ethical and good practice issues in mind. Because couple relationships are so important to adults, children, and society as a whole, affecting our mental health as well as our happiness, any discussion about couple therapy should include the need for therapists' consistent observance of the ethical codes adopted by professional bodies and associations. Those who seek a therapist's help put themselves in a relatively vulnerable position and the therapist bears a consequent responsibility not to exploit their need.

An ethical principle underlies all therapies in response to the question 'What is its aim?' Therapists should acknowledge their own assumptions about the outcome they favour, and be ready to put them aside to consider what resolution is both possible and desirable for the couple. Chapter 11, 'Outcomes: Endings and new beginnings', discusses these questions while recognising the place in all therapy of endings and new beginnings.

TWO IMPORTANT EXPLANATIONS TO GUIDE THE READER

1. *Couple stories and case examples*: vignettes, or short accounts, of couple stories are used in several chapters to illustrate points made. No confidentiality has been breached by their use since, although all include elements of real experience, these are composite stories which do not relate to actual couples.

2. *Words and why they matter*: this book cannot claim to be 'jargon-free', but it aims to be 'jargon-light', and whenever possible to explain terms which refer to specific aspects of couple therapy. The Glossary gives definitions of many of these. Readers will be able to identify such terms because at their first mention in a chapter they are in quotation marks and marked in bold.

'Jargon' – the language used by particular professional groups about aspects of their work – is often difficult for relative outsiders to understand. It may be useful for anyone in the in-group and therefore 'in the know', but it excludes and is unhelpful to others. Writing this book has involved a conscious attempt to avoid making assumptions, although that can be hard. For example, it is important not to assume that terms which we commonly use, and have become 'therapy speak', are universally similarly understood. Language evolves all the time, and differing interpretations of it can readily lead to misunderstanding. The constant risk of this will be familiar to all couples and couple therapists!

SOME DEFINITIONS OF TERMS FREQUENTLY USED IN THIS BOOK

- *Therapy*: for the purposes of this book, 'therapy' is taken to refer to psychological or talking therapies, and not physical or chemically based therapies. Rather than distinguish on each occasion between the different forms of therapies, such as between 'counselling' and 'psychotherapy', 'therapy' is used in a generic way to cover all forms of talking therapies. Sometimes couple therapy is referred to as 'relationship counselling'. A distinction between counselling and psychotherapy is set out in Chapter 4.

- *Couple therapy*: the fact that couple therapy is now an everyday term marks profound changes in today's society. When counselling for couples first emerged some eighty years ago, it was known as 'marital counselling' or 'marriage guidance'. While not all couples then were married, marriage was considered the norm to uphold.

  It is also essential to be clear about who we are talking about when we speak of a *couple*. Chapter 2 addresses this and the different kinds and compositions of couple relationships. This is followed in Chapter 3, by considering the most common reasons for couples' unhappiness.

  In addition, the term 'couple therapy', which is more accepted in the UK, is used throughout in preference to 'couples therapy' which is more usual in the USA. The singular 'couple' is chosen to make it compatible with the singular use of 'child', 'adult', 'individual', and 'family' in relation to therapy. The term 'couple therapy' means different things to different people. What we mean by 'therapy' and the differences between the main forms of therapy available to couples are summarised in Chapters 4 and 6.

- *Work:* therapy is often described as 'work' and, as noted above, a therapeutic relationship as a 'working relationship'. This acknowledges the unique and painstaking tasks involved in assisting couples to understand their feelings about their relationship which, in turn, can lead to changes in behaviour towards one another. Commitment on the part of both the couple and the therapist is needed to apply hopes and energies to this work when it might feel tempting to take a holiday instead. While it can seem very hard work, where there is a will there may also be a way.

- *Diversity*: had this book been written seventy or more years ago, the writer may well have made the general assumption that 'couple' meant 'man and wife' – i.e., that couples are heterosexual, generally married, and patriarchally led: e.g., 'Mr and Mrs Thomas Smith'. There may also have been some recognition that while this was not universally correct, such a generalisation would have felt acceptable. We can no longer do so! Although there was then some diversity in couples, we have only to take stock of the law to see a revolution in society's acceptance of different forms of couple relationships. There is recognition not only that the old heterosexual stereotypes no longer fit, but they also discriminate against making therapy available to all who may need and be otherwise able to use it. Moreover, the range of expressions of gender and of couple relationships themselves has become so wide that the very concept of 'normality' is now the subject of continual questioning.

Acknowledgement of diversity is often seen in the inclusive term 'LGBTQIA+'. Here, this inclusive term, which itself is continually evolving, is covered by the acronym GSRD – gender, sexual, and relationship diverse/diversity – as used by the British Psychoanalytic Council (BPC) and the British Association for Counsellors and Psychotherapists (BACP). A useful bibliography citing books on this issue has been produced by BPC (2023). (See also Campbell, 2023).

- *Pronouns*: where it helps to avoid confusion, and the gender of the person described is relevant, 'he' / 'him' or 'she' / 'her' are used. Otherwise, when the question of gender is not at issue, and in order not to favour one over another, non-binary pronouns – 'they' / 'them' – are used.

FURTHER LEARNING

To take the reader forward in discovering more, Chapter 13 considers the importance of and what can be gained from taught courses about couple therapy.

This is complemented by two Appendices listing links to:

1. Research in couple therapy
2. Organisations promoting further learning

The expanded Bibliography lists not only sources referenced in each chapter, but also additional recommendations of books on skills, and a list of some of the current journals in the field. As well as more academic titles, there are also suggestions for further insights to be found in novels, poetry, TV and films, which offer continually thought-provoking perspectives on couples and their relationships. Thinking about couples is an essential part of couple therapy; as we consider others' representations of couples, we reflect on our own experience and may then see their therapy with new eyes. The artistic world is rich with opportunities for learning and refreshment.

LET US ASK OURSELVES ...

To begin at the beginning, ask yourself:

- What is it about me that makes couple therapy so interesting to me?

And, we might ask:

- If therapy has become relatively 'normalised', why, for so many troubled couples, is *couple* therapy so frequently seen as a last resort, and often only considered at a point when the desired solution is difficult to find?

CHAPTER SUMMARY

- This chapter offers a general introduction to the book, setting out its aims and a brief guide to the contents of its chapters and appendices.
- Stressing the importance of readers' curiosity, the chapter discusses why couple relationships matter so much and what the place of couple therapy is, its relationship, skills, theoretical, ethical, and sexual dimensions, before explaining the composite use of case examples, as well as exploring the use of associated language, such as 'therapy' itself, 'work', and 'diversity'.
- As with all of the book's chapters, readers are left with questions inviting them to enquire further.

REFERENCES

British Psychoanalytic Council (BPC) (2023). Bibliography on Gender, Sexuality and Relationship Diversity. Retrieved 8.3.2024 from: www.bpc.org.uk/?s=GSRD+Bibliography.
Campbell, C. (2023). *Sex Therapy: The Basics*. London: Routledge.

2

WHAT IS A COUPLE?

INTRODUCTION

This chapter discusses the importance of therapists being able to consider the question 'What is a couple?' in an open-minded way, not least because there are no simple answers. The place of the couple in the mind, the family, and society are then addressed, together with belief systems about romantic commitmment. The chapter goes on to compare couple relationships with other close pairs or dyads and stresses the increase in preference for the right to self-definition rather than aspiring to fit a given indentity. The many needs and hopes that would-be couples seek to fulfil in becoming a couple are described, as well as the issues of dependence, codependence, and the contribution of a developmental perspective.

WHAT IS A COUPLE? AN ESSENTIAL AND DECEPTIVELY SIMPLE QUESTION

Although asking 'What is a couple?' is especially important for couple therapists, the more we think about it, the more evident it is that this question has no simple answers. But therapists' readiness to think about it is their first step on the road to being able to engage, with an open mind, with the difficulties that couples bring.

COUPLE AND COUPLES

> Come live with me and be my love,
> And we will all the pleasures prove

Christopher Marlowe (1564–1593)
'The Passionate Shepherd to His Love', published 1600.

DOI: 10.4324/9781003313403-2

Straightaway, we can see clearly what was in Marlowe's mind when he thought about a future alongside his love. Even today, his poem may ring bells with many lovers and would-be lovers. But his words do not necessarily describe what being a couple brings to everyone's mind. This is where definitions in response to asking 'What is a couple?' are both important and unhelpful.

- They are *important* because, so far as couple therapy is concerned, this question lies at the heart of the whole process. As discussed in Chapter 9, one of the most illuminating questions therapists might ask themselves on beginning work with two new clients seeking help is, 'In what ways are these two people a couple?'
- They are *unhelpful* because as soon as we try to pin down a simple definition of a couple, we realise that language is limiting. People are complex and the relationships they make reflect their complexities.

The couple therapist finds answers to the question 'What is a couple?' by walking around it, and viewing couple relationships from a number of different perspectives, such as:

- The couple in the mind.
- The couple in the family.
- The couple in society.

The Couple in the Mind

Marlowe's poem is often quoted, even after almost 500 years, because it still expresses what many people have in mind when thinking about being one of a couple. But if we were to ask 100 people across the world to say what comes to mind when asked to picture a couple, we might be surprised by the number of different images they suggest. They might picture couples they know – perhaps from their families, or celebrity couples, couples from myths or popular fiction, couples who are real or imaginary – or a mix of both, couples wildly in love, or with daggers drawn.

In fact, the kinds of couples we have in our minds, whether we are conscious of these images or not, are enormously important in shaping our expectations of our lives. For this reason, readers are invited to consider the couple in *their* minds as they reflect on ideas raised in this book. As a concept, 'the couple in the mind' has become particularly important to psychodynamic and psychoanalytic ways of thinking about and practising couple therapy. A therapist and writer from this school, Mary Morgan, has coined a term 'a couple state of mind' to describe a way of thinking about couples' relationships which can be developed by couples and therapists alike (Morgan, 2001). It is a way of perceiving the relationship that holds it in mind and recognises its ability to grow. (See also Chapters 4–6).

The Couple in the Family

Couples are given a central place in families. Of course, in any one family, there may be several couples. In coming together, the partners bring with them their own families of origin. This means that they bring with them new relationships, and the possibility for the family of seeing itself from a different perspective. As partners, they can offer a strong alliance with which to meet the challenges the wider family inevitably faces in change and loss. How they manage difficulties matters; it offers a model to be valued or avoided by other family members. Couples can be a strong core in the family, holding it together. As such, the couple in the family could be thought of as an 'organising principle'. By the same token, the fallout, if the couple separates, can lead to major splits and divided loyalties which may take at least a generation to heal. Their uncoupling signals that something on which others have depended can be irreparably broken. It chimes with the sense of trauma evoked in W.B. Yeats' poem 'The Second Coming' (1920).

> Things fall apart; the centre cannot hold;
> Mere anarchy is loosed upon the world,
> The blood-dimmed tide is loosed, and everywhere
> The ceremony of innocence is drowned;
> The best lack all conviction, while the worst
> Are full of passionate intensity.

The complexity and significance of the couple's place in the family is increased if and when the couple become parents, an event which creates many new relationships. The couple then also becomes a parental couple, and even if the couple decides to separate, the parental couple relationship endures, with aspects of it living on in the couple and the minds of the couple's children.

The Couple in Society

It could be argued that couples and families are given a pivotal role in society. The state of their welfare might be seen as a bellwether of social wellbeing. Opinions about what kinds of couple relationships are socially acceptable have changed radically in the past 100 years. Perhaps the biggest change is that to be fully accepted as a couple, partners do not need to be married, nor be in a civil partnership, although the legal rights of those whose relationship is not recognised in that way may vary from country to country. Civil partnership for same-sex couples became legally recognised in the UK in 2005. In the USA, the legal status of civil unions or 'domestic partnerships' varied from state to state, a situation which was mostly resolved in 2015 by the nationwide legalisation of same-sex marriage. The history of marriage as a legally binding and/or entitling contract is set out by Lennon (2023).

Nowadays, too, there is increasing acceptance of couples who come from diverse racial, religious, or cultural backgrounds, as well as greater recognition of partners who are same-sex or transgender, and of intimate relationships with multiple partners. Older concepts of norms are eroding as a diversity in couples' relationships arrangements becomes accepted and normalised. This makes it all the more important for a therapist to check regularly their assumptions on GSRD matters, and not to assume that a couple's happiness is derived from their conformity to a model (McCann, 2022). Any assumptions the partners may have are, of course, a different but important matter.

TRYING DEFINITIONS FOR SIZE

Thus, when trying to define 'couple', we see that this one word covers many meanings. Indeed, definitions are no longer the preserve of the law or lexicographers. Increasingly, people now define themselves, finding a multitude of terms and ways to express their individuality and identity. Whatever is published is likely to be soon, if not already, out of date. Therapists must be sensitive to what couples are telling them; is their relationship seeking to conform to a notional norm, or to be essentially non-conformist? Are they seeking an outsider's view, or to establish the right to self-definition?

However a couple describes their relationship, seen in the context of couple therapy, couples are more than simply two people. Like the couple Marlowe longed for, they are seen as having a strong enough link between them to form a shared understanding. This will be the basis for them to co-create a relationship that each hopes will meet their needs. In other words, they can be mutually dependent. The couple has also evolved into being a new entity: two people *plus* a relationship – a kind of threesome.

Seeing them as two people plus a relationship clearly *also* describes other twosome relationships, or dyads, such as siblings, parents and children, close friendships, or business partners. While we might call these 'dyads', do couple relationships need further definition?

SOME POSSIBLE DISTINGUISHING FEATURES

- *Romance*: whether it is instant or potential, romance is generally considered a vital ingredient. Dyads and couple relationships may have much in common; for example, mutual dependency, experience of living together, a shared – sometimes unspoken – language, sharing confidences, and trust. For dyads, however, romance is not on the cards. A 'bromance' is an interesting example of this, being a close platonic (i.e., non-sexual) relationship between two men. Romance conjures up ideas of excitement, love, idealisation, mystery, and sexual attraction. As a result, romance is also *not* expected between other pairs in families; indeed it would cross the taboo of incest.

   Couples therefore differ because, for them, there is usually an expectation of a romantic involvement. By 'romantic', I am referring to the sparks of attraction, both physical and psychological, which thrill and enliven the couple's experience of being together and thinking about one another. These may not be exclusive to one partner – see below – nor do they define all loving, committed couples.

But/and – additional important exceptions:

- *Non-sexual couples*: we should note that feelings of physical attraction and idealisation of one another, so much part of falling in love, may change over time, as a result of many factors. But those early feelings also help couples to hold on to and develop their love for one another.
- *Celibate or asexual couples*: examples of the above may be couples who mutually prefer asexuality; e.g., same-sex couples in religious organisations whose union is recognised on condition that they are celibate.
- *Arranged marriages*: couples, who come together following a family or other arrangement, rather than their own independent choice, also say that romance and love can grow between them; they 'walk into' love rather than 'fall in love' (Kapur, 2023).
- *Friendship – couple relationship continuum*: close friendships – sometimes even called 'bosom pals' – can develop into couple relationships, and over time couple relationships can lose romance and sexual contact, while remaining close companionable friendships. Being close and companionable, however, is not to say that there are never passionate rows or differences; far from it. But being able to tolerate differences while remaining in a close friendship is a valued part of a lasting couple relationship (Harrison, 2022).
- *Romantic non-monogamy*: couple therapists are increasingly asked to consider issues raised by people who are in relationships which they describe as consensual non-monogamy (CNM) or ethically non-monogamous (ENM). These are intimate romantic relationships, often referred to as polyamorous, which involve more than two people at a time; e.g., a 'throuple', a triad, or a 'quad' – when two couples combine together polyamorously. Previously such couples may have described this as a 'ménage à trois' or an 'open relationship' (McCann, 2022).

- *Degrees of separation?*: some couples need to be separate – e.g.,
  - *'Living together apart'*: couples who are emotionally and possibly sexually close, but who, for a number of reasons, physically live separately – e.g., in long-distance relationships.
  - *'Living apart together'*: couples who are emotionally and sexually distant, but share the same household.
- *Some couples need conflict*: some partners are drawn together by their needs to work out traumatic experiences. They develop sadomasochistic relationships which may be both verbally and physically violent and abusive. Despite continual quarrelling and seeking to hurt one another, they are mutually dependent; each needs the other as a particular partner with whom to fight, without ever 'having it out' to settle their arguments.

WHAT CONCLUSIONS CAN WE DRAW?

- *Definitions are important, but/and beware generalisations*: superficial assumptions can suppose couple relationships to be generally close, intimate, loving. While this may be true for many, any kind of generalisation is unhelpful and, in the end, discriminatory, because it fails to take account of the important reasons why people make and stay in couple relationships.
- *Finding a mate is popular but/and not all adults are in couple relationships*: it is estimated that in the UK and USA, broadly two thirds of adults are in relationships, with one third remaining single. It also seems that in the UK more adults are postponing getting into settled relationships until their 30s, and they are also having fewer children, later in life.

  For precise statistics for the UK on this, see rates of marriage and divorce (Office for National Statistics, 2021; National Records of Scotland, 2013). An understanding of population trends is helpful in offering insight about what couples may consider to be norms for relationships amongst their peers, as well as in their families of origin.

Where Does a Relationship Start?

Is it with a wish – whether we are aware of wanting it or not – to find a mate? Or is it with an encounter – such as in the 1958 film

South Pacific 'across a crowded room' – when the trigger of attraction was pulled? Psychotherapists, social scientists, and neurologists have long debated what *attraction* is made of. What draws one person to another? Looks? Behaviour? Wealth? Or something less easily defined, summed up mysteriously as 'chemistry'?

Psychoanalytically speaking, the concept of '**projection**' offers a useful image. When looking for someone to love (whether or not we are aware of looking), projection happens when we seek someone onto whom we can project or bestow qualities which we ourselves would like. These qualities are attractive because they seem to match or complement our own attributes and thus make up for what we might imagine as being missing or insufficient in ourselves. Thus, seeking a mate feels like a search for completion. When the 'feeling is mutual' and the relationship is strengthened by mutual projections, the bond between the two is described by psychodynamic–psychoanalytic therapists as a '**couple fit**'. Some couples refer to one another as 'my better half', as if, with all the projections, their partner has come to embody part of themself. The reverse of this dynamic, of course, also has its downside; when couples uncouple, to disengage they often project onto one another negative feelings and failings they might have seen in themselves. They are thus still attached and, to complete the disengagement, paradoxically, these negative projections will have, in time, to be withdrawn and reclaimed.

WHAT MIGHT KEEP A RELATIONSHIP GOING?

After falling for one another, what do couples need to help their relationship grow stronger? Some would argue, that like the first chance encounter, a lot of luck is involved. But more relevant questions for couple therapists might concern what belief systems underlie the kinds of relationships that adults make. Psychoanalytic and Jungian thinkers have written extensively about this (see Chapter 7).

Psychologists have recently described two categories of couples whose fundamental beliefs about relationships greatly influence whether they fall into or fall out of staying together. These beliefs have been summed up (Knee, 1998) as:

- '*Romantic destiny*': the belief that partners are either basically compatible or they are not. So if at first a relationship does not succeed, there is no point in trying again to make it work; or

- *'Romantic growth'*: the belief that relationships can improve with time because difficulties can be worked out to strengthen couples staying together.

These beliefs about relationships also appear to affect couples' attitudes towards their sexual relationships; they are either fatalistic if there are difficulties on the first night, or consider them worth sticking with on the assumption that where there's a loving will, there's a way (Maxwell et al., 2016). How these assumptions are also influenced by the earlier lives of partners is discussed in Chapter 7.

So Why Be a Couple?

How do we make sense of the enduring place that couples have in human longing? Their starring or pivotal roles in fiction, film, plays, and poetry place them at the heart of human hopes and relationships. We only have to be reminded of the popularity of romantic fiction to know how powerful the concept of coupling up is. Whether the hope is realistic or not, for many the idea of being in a couple relationship expresses so many of our ideals. Sigmund Freud observed that the first couple we make is with our mother. If the urge to be part of a couple is born with us, that urge generally becomes stronger as we grow up. What needs does it meet? Essentially, they fall under one heading:

Dependence

Ronald Fairbairn, a child and adult psychiatrist and psychoanalyst, saw dependence as part of the developmental journey that we all must make. In his terms, we start from complete dependence as a babe in arms and progress as adults to 'mature dependence'. To achieve mature dependence, it is essential to be able to rely on making and developing relationships with others. Thus, from being totally dependent on our parents or other carers, gradually our dependence is widened out and eventually it rests in culture and society. True maturity may not therefore be achieved by becoming independent, but by recognising that we can be both autonomous (self-governing) and accepting of mutual dependence on others.

As with degrees of separation noted above, there are also degrees of dependence. Being part of a couple expresses the wish to be dependent on another in various ways – emotionally, sexually, physically, financially – but the degree to which one partner is dependent on the other in any of these aspects will vary, and may vary over time in any one couple.

There is a further relationship between dependence and separation: in adult life, mutually dependent relationships paradoxically only survive when they allow partners to be separate.

Being mutually dependent means being able to express and share needs. 'Codependency' is a term increasingly used to describe an imbalance between partners in expressing and meeting needs. In codependent relationships, there is an implicit understanding that one partner will negate their own emotional needs to prioritise the wants and desires of the other.

NEEDS COMMONLY SOUGHT IN COUPLE RELATIONSHIPS

The following list, which is not comprehensive, shows that many needs are interrelated. They are not ranked in order of priority; that would require a subjective judgment which only those involved can make. What they have in common is *intercourse*, i.e., something that ebbs and flows between two people *which may or may not be sexual*.

- *The need to feel loved*: to be noticed, listened to, know you are important to the one you love. These needs go hand in hand with:
- *To have your love accepted* by the one you love. And this relates to needing:
- *To belong*: a good part of attraction has to do with belonging. The psychoanalyst Jock Sutherland described the universal power of a wish to be 'somebody's somebody'. This is similar to wanting to be part of a relationship in which we are put first, and of course is close to the desire to be able to put our trust in someone, as well as to needs:
- *For sexual satisfaction, compatibility, and trust*: while sexual compatibility may or may not happen instantly, for many couples the sense that their own sexual bond is special to them, allows

them to trust one another physically and to trust that their relationship can exclude others.

- *To share life with someone who accepts one's sexuality*: an aspect of identity in which many feel vulnerable.
- *To mature*: most romantic fiction, like myths and fables before it, shows couples being presented with challenges to be overcome before they can realise the dream of 'living happily ever after'. A couple relationship offers an arena in which our ideals, and with them ourselves and our partner, can be put to the test. And dreams can be tested against reality.
- *To express and discover oneself*: when we make a relationship with another, we can learn more about our own identity as well as about theirs. We create a play in which we are both lead and supporting actor. When both partners are content to co-write the script, the play can last their lifetimes. This all depends on them being able to be co-directors – to talk together about their shared lives and about what matters to them. This is closely associated with a need:
- *To work out previous relationship difficulties*: the choice of partner may be influenced by the shared unconscious wish to find solutions to family conflict and distress passed down through generations or instilled through childhood deprivation or abuse.
- *To play together*: spending time with someone with whom you can laugh, relax, be quiet, play music, or entertain enriches both partners and increases mutual trust. The saying 'The family that plays together stays together' could also be applied to couples because play is a vital part of our creative lives from infancy onwards.
- *To fight together*: love and hate can be close companions, as previously mentioned. It is important to be able to be real about our anger and what we hate and to do so safely without needlessly hurting or being hurt.
- *To make a 'secure base' for a family*: if children are desired, we might look for someone with whom to create a home for them. Chapter 8 also considers the therapeutic context of a '**secure base**'. This is close to the need:
- *For security – to be looked after*: the marriage vows, which promise commitment 'in sickness and in health' underline the need

to depend on a partner, to be able to be vulnerable despite adversity.

- *To escape*: a partner might offer us a way of escaping loneliness, an abusive family, or feeling stuck by thwarted ambitions.
- *To fit in*: the 'fear of missing out' (FOMO) covers a range of anxieties about not conforming to what one's peers are doing and enjoying and so appearing different.

So What Helps a Couple Stay Together?

When enough of the needs listed above are met to give each partner enough satisfaction, it will buy them time to collaborate as a couple to work out difficulties which come with major life stresses, e.g., illness, loss of work, poverty, and death in the family. In this way, partners may grow to understand, without necessarily being consciously aware of it, that there are times when their relationship needs time and patience, rather than high expectations.

Can Couple Relationships Grow?

They can be seen to grow and develop with their own life cycles. That couples' relationships are affected by partners' external circumstances as well as their emotional states is not remarkable. Just as individual partners' lives are affected by the arrival of children, or losing a parent, or moving into middle age and/or retirement, so too are the shared lives of couples, which are seen to pass through phases as the couple share the joys and challenges that each life stage presents. Thinking about the ways in which the couple relationship adapts is termed a 'developmental perspective'. Developmental issues are considered further in Chapter 10.

LET US ASK OURSELVES ...

- How have your ideas about the question 'What is a couple?' changed in the last ten years?
- What has been most influential for you in making any change?
- Are there any kinds of couples you would not feel comfortable working with? Why?

CHAPTER SUMMARY

- The importance of asking 'What is a couple?' is discussed, arguing for therapists' critical capacities to have an open-minded approach; while definitions are important, generalisation is unhelpful.
- The place of the couple in the mind, the family, and society is considered, along with belief systems about what romantic commitmment means.
- Couples' relationships are compared with those of other close dyads noting an increasing preference for self-definition instead of given indentity; issues such as dependence and growth are also covered.
- Needs of would-be couples and the beliefs which may underlie their hopes are described.

HAVE YOU READ?

Byatt, A.S. (1990). *Possession*. London: Chatto & Windus.

Finkel, E. (2017). *The All-or-Nothing Marriage*. Boston: E.P. Dutton.

Greer, A.S. (2008). *The Story of a Marriage*. London: Faber & Faber.

McEwan, I. (2007). *On Chesil Beach*. London: Jonathan Cape.

REFERENCES AND FILMOGRAPHY

Harrison, J. (2022). *Five Arguments All Couples (Need To) Have*. London: Profile Books.

Kapur, S. (dir.) (2023). *What's Love Got to Do with It?* [film]. StudioCanal UK.

Knee, C.R. (1998). Implicit Theories of Relationships: Assessment and Prediction of Romantic Relationship Initiation. *Journal of Personality and Social Psychology*, 74(2), 360–370.

Lennon, R. (2023). *Wedded Wife: A Feminist History of Marriage*. London: Aurum Press.

Logan, J. (dir.) (1958). *South Pacific* [film]. 20th Century Studios.

McCann, D. (ed.) (2022). *Same-Sex Couples and Other Identities*. London: Routledge.

Marlowe, C. (1600). The Passionate Shepherd to His Love. In: R. Clay (ed.) (1862). *Poets of the Elizabethan Age* (pp. 21–22). London: Sampson Lowe and Co.

Maxwell, J.A., Muise, A., MacDonald, G., Day, L.C., Rosen, N.O., & Impett, E.A. (2016). How Implicit Theories of Sexuality Shape Sexual and Relationship Well-Being. *Journal of Personality and Social Psychology*, 112(2), 238–279.

Morgan, M. (2001). First Contacts: The 'Couple State of Mind' as a Factor in the Containment of Couples Seen for Initial Consultations. In: F. Grier (ed.) *Brief Encounters with Couples* (pp.17–32). London: Karnac.

National Records of Scotland (2013). Population Estimates by Marital Status for Scotland. Retrieved 29.11.2023 from: https://www.data.gov.uk/dataset/c04cc034-9978-4de8-9116-12ebd3497462/population-estimates-by-marital-status-for-scotland.

Office for National Statistics (2021). Population Estimates by Marital Status and Living Arrangements, England and Wales. Retrieved 29.11.2023 from: https://www.ons.gov.uk/people populationandcommunity/populationandmigration/population estimates/bulletins/populationestimatesbymaritalstatusandliving arrangements/2020.

Yeats, W.B. (1920). The Second Coming. In: *The Collected Poems of W.B. Yeats*. Ware: Wordsworth Editions Ltd.

3

WHY DO COUPLES SEEK THERAPY?

INTRODUCTION

This chapter explores why when their relationship breaks down, couples look to therapy for support. It begins by explaining how internal and external stresses may combine to overwhelm couples to the point of relationship breakdown. In seeking to show how couple therapy is designed specifically to address couples' unhappiness, this chapter is linked closely with the description of couple therapy in Chapter 4. It also suggests why, even though the therapy tries to take account of the many reasons couples give for their distress, unhappy couples do not always seek it out. The chapter goes on to offer ways of organising our understanding of a relationship breakdown's many causes to enable therapists to hold them in mind. There is consideration of what constitutes a 'presenting' problem before discussing what help therapy might provide. The chapter concludes by using William Shakespeare's *Hamlet* as an illustration of sorrows that beset couples, before giving the couple therapist's perspective.

WHY CHOOSE THERAPY?

There are many reasons why couple therapy is *not* for everyone:

- Support is available from family and friends;
- One partner cannot, or is unwilling to, attend, and individual therapy is preferred;
- Good, accessible, affordable couple therapy is not available;
- Fear of recrimination, violent repercussions;
- Shame.

DOI: 10.4324/9781003313403-3

For these reasons, we should not assume that the pain of relationship breakdown will be enough to prompt couples to seek therapy. In fact, compared with the number of couples who break up, those who opt for couple therapy are in a minority. It is possible therefore that for many couples, therapy is tried as a last resort, when all else has failed. Therapists would do well to remember then that, for the couple, this process remains on trial, to be challenged and strength tested. After all, embarking on couple therapy involves a good deal of emotional, as well as some financial, investment, and generally requires a belief from one or both partners that it is going to be worth it.

BELIEFS ABOUT THE VALUE OF THERAPY

Chapter 2 differentiated between beliefs in 'romantic growth' and 'romantic destiny'. The strength of such belief systems is shaped by early experiences. For example, children learn early in life to protect themselves against the disappointment of hopes that were too frequently dashed. Where these beliefs remain strong in adult life, they will clearly influence whether or not couples are prepared to invest in therapy and how willing they will be to tolerate its demands. Couples' and families' beliefs need to be respected rather than dismissed without enquiry; whether or not they are justified, their beliefs have been developed to manage threats to family structures. The couple may not be aware, or only partially aware, of some beliefs – for example, that in close relationships one partner is always dominant and must be placated, or that it is not safe to be too dependent on others because they may leave or abuse you.

SEVEN REASONS FOR CHOOSING COUPLE THERAPY

SEVEN IMPORTANT ASPECTS PERSUADING COUPLES TO CHOOSE THERAPY

1. The outsider's view
2. Sharing the therapy
3. Focussing on the relationship
4. Programming the work
5. Couples are part of a wider circle
6. Crises can be overwhelming
7. Valuing past and present

Supporting arguments for the seven aspects are set out as follows:

1. *The value of an outsider's perspective*: some couples prefer couple therapy's more neutral opinion over opinions given by those close to them. Robert Burns spelled out the power of having the outsider's view:

    > O wad some Power the giftie gie us
    > To see oursels as ithers see us!
    >
    > (Robert Burns, 'To a Louse', published 1985).

2. *A problem shared is … couple therapy*: couple therapy is not necessarily an easy choice, especially as it is often supposed that surely one partner is at fault and should then put things right. But putting right an unhappy relationship is an enormous responsibility to shoulder alone. Given that relationship breakdown is generally multi-causal, stemming from partners' reactions to one another, both have to recognise that their difficulties are shared. If they choose couple therapy to do this, the therapist's role is to hold a space in which both can feel heard. If one partner takes charge and the other opts out, or if one feels held to blame while the other feels always in the right, any 'solution' is unlikely to lead to lasting or greater happiness.

    If, for whatever reason, the couple cannot collaborate, perhaps from fear, or refusal to hear the other's view, then therapy as a couple is clearly not going to prove useful. To have any chance of 'getting off first base', couple therapy needs both partners to commit to attending most sessions together.

3. *The focus is on the relationship*: significantly, early on, when couple therapy was being developed as a separate form of therapy, it was recommended that its focus should be on the *relationship* between the couple, rather than on the two individual partners attending (Dicks, 1967).

4. *Making a date to meet and think*: couple therapy creates a dedicated time and space in which to meet and explore issues which the couple have found too contentious to face alone.

5. *No couple is an island*: borrowing from the poet, John Donne (1624): 'No man is an island, entire of itself …' we can also see that couples are not islands. What affects a couple affects a wide circle of people around them, including children, wider

families, friends, work colleagues, and neighbours. And the difficulties couples experience are not islands either; relationship breakdowns often occur for interrelated reasons. Choosing couple therapy should take all of this into account.

6. *'Sorrows come … in battalions'*: relationship breakdowns happen for a whole range of reasons, some coinciding overwhelmingly. Couples may blame one major problem, but often it is one among many and has become the 'straw' that has broken the back of their relationship. Shakespeare has Claudius in *Hamlet*, say: 'When sorrows come, they come not single spies, but in battalions' (Shakespeare, *Hamlet*, IV: V).

   This allusion to an invasion or war setting seems powerfully appropriate to warring couples. Couple therapy recognises that, for the therapist and couple, exploring relationship breakdown might sometimes be like walking through a minefield – there are so many interlinked 'mines' and 'craters' that it can be hard to anticipate what may trigger further explosions and cause more hurt.

7. *A choice of chicken or egg?*: couples may choose therapy to resolve a particular conflict they have identified. But do couple therapists opt to start by addressing its symptoms or causes? Chapter 6 discusses the different approaches different therapies have to this dilemma. Broadly speaking, some focus on looking with the couple at what are often called the 'here and now' symptoms of their conflict, while others aim to help the couple understand the underlying, long-standing, and even unrecognised, roots of their present difficulties. Drawing a distinction between symptoms and causes is not done here to diminish the significance of either. For example, violence, emotional abuse, and affairs may be regarded as symptoms of underlying relationship difficulties, while at the same time considered to be requiring immediate attention.

LEARNING FROM THE SEVEN SUPPORTING REASONS

Keeping a Thinking Head

Rudyard Kipling has useful advice in his poem 'If': to 'keep your head when all about you are losing theirs' (Kipling, 2020). For couple therapy to be a place where stress and quarrelling can meet calm reflection, the therapist needs to organise their understanding about a couple's problems without also becoming overwhelmed.

Readers will readily connect what follows with descriptions in Chapter 9 of assessment in early meetings with couples.

Seeing Problems in Clusters

Lists of reasons couples give for relationship breakdown can accumulate to as many as thirty. It would be quite overwhelming for any couple therapist to have *all* of them in mind, and while there is a need to be aware of the potential range of reasons, when therapists first meet with a couple it is probable that they will describe one major issue, with the possibility of two or three associated others.

Readers are therefore recommended to envisage these inter-linked issues in clusters, with some appearing in more than one cluster.

FOUR CLUSTERS OF CAUSES

1. Why now?
2. Rejection of difference
3. Betrayal and loss of trust
4. Losses not shared or mourned

'Why Now?'

'Why now?' is a key question for therapists because the timing of crises speaks volumes about what is fundamentally amiss. Tensions, rifts, and pre-existing unresolved differences tend to surface and become less manageable during periods of significant stress and change, e.g., the arrival of children, the illness or death of close family members, societal unrest caused by pandemics or war. In addition, couples today will have experienced phenomenal social changes with the advent of dating apps, and more fluid sexual expectations. While external pressures are very challenging, internal pressures show them to be only part of the story, as is illustrated in Figure 3.1.

Figure 3.1 'Why now?'

Some of the issues contributing to 'Why now?' are further explained as follows:

- *Trauma has a long reach*: experiences of rejection and abuse in childhood, may appear 'buried' but can be re-awakened as couples struggle to mend their separate past hurts together. The dormant dread of being unlovable is brought to light in fears of abandonment, violence, and sexual rejection.

- *Life-cycle issues*: the birth of children, blending of previously separate families, and 'emptying of the parental nest', however much desired, can stir up rivalries and anxieties about being put first. The transition from couple to parents signals a landmark change (Cowan & Cowan, 2000). As explained in Chapter 10, couples' relationships themselves are dynamic and change with age. The significance of any one of the listed causes of distress will depend on the particular age and stage of their relationship.

- *Financial pressures*: money worries surface when family support for child care is geographically distanced, or there is sickness and disability; eviction and homelessness may follow. Depending on parents' resilience, and how earlier life enabled them to manage loss and adversity, some couples find themselves more vulnerable to conflict, depression, loneliness, self-medication with alcohol, or even violence and petty crime. Early support from couple therapy could help to prevent such chain reactions, although sufficient access to it is often restricted by the availability of affordable services (Balfour et al., 2012).

  Failure to negotiate about separate and shared financial resources can become a significant source of conflict (Strober & Davisson, 2023). Why do couples struggle to talk frankly about money? Perhaps having money represents an ability to be self-sufficient, or not having it risks being dependent on one's partner. Talking about it together may raise wider questions about how safe it is to be dependent on someone or to accept them being dependent on you.

- *The impact of external stresses*: societal pressures may make couple relationships stronger in meeting the challenge together, or may prove to be too great a test. For example, research following the COVID-19 pandemic (Usher et al., 2020; Galdiolo et al., 2022) shows that being 'locked down' together proved a make-or-break test for many couples. Although some enjoyed spending more time together, in England and Wales, the divorce rate increased by almost 10% following the first lockdown of 2020–2021 (Office for National Statistics, Census, 2021).

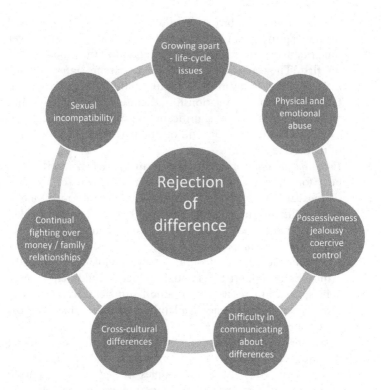

Figure 3.2 Rejection of difference

Rejection of Difference

Much current interest in partners' difficulties in accepting and valuing one another's differences (see Figure 3.2) is sometimes thought about in terms of '**narcissism**' (See Chapters 7 and 10), and often in terms of understanding physical and emotional violence. If one partner's anxiety is heightened by the loss of control in the world at large, this may lead to a wish to take control of relationships at home. In its mildest form, this anxiety may appear in continual nagging or reminders to correct behaviour. At its most severe, it may be violent, and is seen as '**coercive control**', which was designated a crime in the UK in 2015. Increasingly recognised as a feature of malignant couple relationships, it may occur in both heterosexual and same-sex relationships. In the case of coercive control, control is sought with regard to everything the partner does, says and thinks, such that they are afraid to be themselves. Most reported controllers are male, with women predominantly more passive.

Worryingly, there now appears to be a universally recorded increase in intimate partner violence and homicide, and it has been estimated that about a quarter of couples seeking divorce cite physical or emotional abuse as their reason. Many couples who are affected do not seek therapy for fear of the consequences of making this public. To counter this, some have used social media to raise 'red flags', highlighting the need for awareness that such aggression or the coincidence of too many transgressions should not be tolerated.

Figure 3.3 Betrayal and loss of trust

Betrayal and Loss of Trust

Couples often seek therapy after one or both of them has had an affair or affairs. The loss of trust in a partner leads to a sense of betrayal and of feeling abandoned (see Figure 3.3); these are often seen as causes of relationship breakdown, but may equally be thought of as symptoms, as discussed in Chapter 9. Loss of trust, arising from feelings of abandonment, may also coincide with a perceived withdrawal by one partner due to, for instance, pregnancy or depression. But as Figure 3.4 also illustrates, feeling abandoned may be triggered by many circumstances. Exposing the full meaning of the betrayal may thus be both important and fraught with danger.

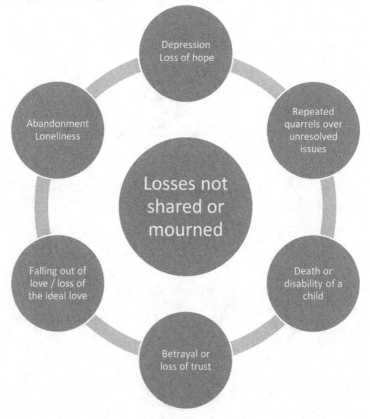

Figure 3.4 Losses not shared or mourned

Losses not Shared or Mourned

Couples' difficulties in supporting one another through loss and grief prove a major stumbling block. When they seek therapy, they may not always have recognised that this may be at the core of what has broken between them. The loss of mutual support not only means that their relationship is unable to grow, but that isolation and resentment build in its place.

Death or disability in a child is a particularly painful source of shared guilt and pain. Sometimes one partner is less able than the other to recognise or express empathy or grief.

'Stuckness' or a 'broken record' experience is often significant. Generally, what has caused a breakdown is not the quarrel, fight, or stand-off the couple report they have just had. On closer enquiry, they are often caught up in the same repeated fight. Couples need to be able to fight – to quarrel and make up so they can find ways of expressing healthy differences and negotiate how to live with them (Harrison, 2022). But repeated failure to resolve conflict leads to repeated wrangling and the underlying meaning of their unhappiness remains unexplored. However, fighting has hidden benefits too. Joining a fight may be preferable to grieving together. And fighting can push issues, such as acceptance of each other's difference and negotiating about money, out of reach.

SO WHERE DO WE START?

WITH 'PROBLEMS' OR 'SORROWS'?

The four clusters of causes may not be exhaustive, but registering their complexity may feel exhausting. It is little wonder then that couples' difficulties are often termed 'problems' – perhaps enabling us all to distance ourselves from feeling the pain they arouse. Thinking about them instead as 'sorrows' is more empathically appropriate.

Above, in Figures 3.1–3.4, these sorrows are shown linked together, as if 'in battalions'. So, just as falling *in* love is a process of embracing a wealth of positives, with one assumption leading to several promising others, falling *out* of love is a process in which faith and trust in the one-time lover progressively disintegrates and fragments, leaving a sense of emptiness. In seeking couple therapy, couples may be hoping that they can be helped to make sense of so much sorrow by someone who can imaginatively and empathically 'join the dots'.

WITH THE 'PRESENTING PROBLEM' AND/OR OTHER PROBLEMS?

Bearing in mind how the sorrows that overwhelm us come 'in battalions', it may seem a paradox that couples who seek therapy often say that they need help for *one* major reason. Therapists often describe that reason as the 'presenting problem'. But whatever it is, that problem has never arrived alone. At the very least, it comes with another – i.e., that the couple's relationship has been unable to help them to work out their problem together without an outsider's help. This means that it is highly likely that the 'presenting problem' is a cloak behind which other, as yet unresolved difficulties, such as those in the clusters illustrated above, are sheltering.

Nevertheless, it will be important empathically to start at the couple's starting point, even while anticipating that what is presented is not necessarily 'an open and shut case'.

WITH A SENSE OF PERSPECTIVE?

Now that we have been able to weigh up couples' motivations for avoiding and seeking therapy, along with their ambivalence, it is easier to understand why belief in its value runs the gauntlet of several challenges. Putting their faith in something that may fail, just as their relationship has failed them, is perhaps the greatest obstacle for couples. They are understandably ready to put up barriers against speaking openly about their difficulties. In the light of the complexity of the factors that lead to breakdown and break-up, it is worth reviewing the reasons that hold couples back from committing to a process of therapy. We may now better understand feelings such as shame, fear, loss, hopelessness, and resistance to change in the following ways:

- *Shame*: about airing private fears and feelings; 'washing dirty linen in public'; being thought guilty of failure at making relationships and thus unlovable; sexual rejection; loss of face.

- *Fear*: of retribution from a partner's emotional or physical violence; making a bad situation worse; being found wanting; saying hurtful, harmful things; losing a sense of self-sufficiency and control.
- *Loss*: giving up what has been shared; acknowledging losses not yet mourned together; letting go of hope.
- *Hopelessness*: doubts about whether help is possible. Couples may ask for a therapist's help, but therapists should not assume they really want or expect to receive it.
- *Resistance to change*: all of the above encourages couples, whether as separate partners or together, to cling to fixed beliefs that are resistant to change.

TOLERATING THE PAIN OF BEING IN TWO MINDS?

When therapy is considered a last resort, it may be that by that time, difficulties and hurt will seem to present too big a hurdle. It is crucial that therapists recognise the power of couples' fears that their therapy will prove ineffective and that break-up is inevitable. Indeed, the task of the therapy may be to enable that to happen as equably as possible. It means that the therapist will need to be able to hold two states of mind. In one, there is place for the hope of reconciliation, however fragile, that the couple may bring; while in the other, there is acceptance that their future wellbeing may require them to separate.

STEPPING BACK AND TAKING STOCK

HOW MIGHT A COUPLE THERAPIST MAKE SENSE OF ALL OF THIS?

Because this question is so central to couple therapy, the reader is invited to pursue it more fully in further chapters:

- Chapter 4 looks at what constitutes couple therapy.
- Chapter 5 examines the basic skills used.
- Chapter 9 considers the processes of assessment.

Here, however, there is a renewed emphasis on the value of asking questions. Couples may come to therapy seeking to make statements – especially angry ones – but underneath them are many unanswered questions: Why me? Why us? Why now? A natural response would be to try to offer couples an immediate answer – as if the answer is obvious, or even as if an answer is what is wanted. There may be no single answer; it may be more important that the question is heard.

The therapist's ability to continue to ask themselves questions creates an open space for exploration and discovery. The following questions are echoed in Chapters 5 and 9, but are worth flagging up here for the therapist to hold in mind:

- Am I ready for anything?
- What is not being said?
- What am I at risk of not seeing?
- Can I offer an appropriate setting for meeting?

CONCLUSIONS – AN EPILOGUE

The tragic story of Hamlet's family may help to draw the threads of these ideas together. *Hamlet*, so often seen in terms of an individual's crisis, can also usefully illustrate a couple's and a family's tragedy. In the play, Claudius speaks about 'sorrows' to his new wife, Gertrude, who, until recently, was his sister-in-law. This couple certainly faces an overwhelming sea of problems; the immediate or 'presenting' one is the mental breakdown of Ophelia, a young woman at their court. Ophelia's grief is for her dead father, who has been killed by Gertrude's son, Hamlet, the prince with whom Ophelia is in love. Hamlet has fled the country.

Needless to say, Claudius and Gertrude's marriage belongs to dramatic fiction, not real life. Yet there are aspects of their story that do feature in the distress that often brings couples into therapy today. Claudius and Gertrude are not, of course, seeking couple therapy, but if we were to put the audience in a prospective couple therapist's role, we can see that the difficulties their relationship has to deal with are now descending on them 'in battalions'. Our imaginary therapist has already learned that their marriage followed an affair which led to Claudius secretly murdering Gertrude's husband, Hamlet's father. The couple's enormous burdens of guilt and loss have spilled over to affect and infect the family, preventing them from moving forward. Hamlet, the heir to their throne, has inherited the overwhelming problems which they are struggling to address. He plays out their stuckness through his paralysing depression, which has left him unable to embark on his adult post-university life as a prince, a lover, and a friend.

HIGHLIGHTING THE KEY FACTORS

- *Fall-out from an affair*: whether or not the couple involved in the affair then stay together, their family and friends who act as the supporting frame around them, are affected, as is everyone who is aware of it. The range of their responses, such as feelings of betrayal, dismay, and conflicted loyalties, shows that trust in family relationships will have been shaken and will take time to be restored. Children are particularly affected and, whether they are children or adults, they may become so distressed that their behaviour causes their parents to seek help for them. Claudius' murderous plot against Hamlet, was not at all helpful, but in reality, sensitive children's services will often recognise that it is the parental couple who is in most need of help and so a referral for couple therapy may result from this.

  So far as the couple is concerned, the hurt resulting from one partner's affair frequently prevents them from realising that having an affair is a way for one partner to communicate to, or to enact, something that could not be put into words.
- *'Communication difficulties'*: this frequently used term tries to sum up the range of difficulties that frustrate partners in negotiating their needs. Intercourse, psychologically and sexually (see Chapter 2), has broken down; this may be due to a wish to avoid raising painful issues involving guilt or loss.
- *Loss*: losses that remain insufficiently mourned create open wounds in couple relationships. Loss occurs not only after death, but also following illness – mental or physical – and mutual trust is lost after family breakdown. If there have been several losses, as each remains unmourned, they become cumulative and overwhelming.

- *Depression*: the state of mind of one or both partners can be debilitating, even if it has not been formally diagnosed as 'clinically depressed'. Often, however, affected partners complain of frustration or of a lack of communication (Hewison, Clulow, and Drake, 2014). When there is a withdrawal from one another, the widening gap may be unconsciously filled with partners' negative suppositions (Bion, 1962).

LET US ASK OURSELVES ...

- From all the possible causes for relationship breakdown, which do you think are particularly damaging?
- Which issues would you find it most challenging to work with?

CHAPTER SUMMARY

- This chapter explores why couples may or may not look to therapy for support when their relationship falls apart.
- The causes of relationship breakdown are organised into four interlinked clusters which are each discussed.
- The starting points for therapy are considered along with what constitutes a 'presenting' problem.
- Shakespeare's *Hamlet* is used to illustrate how internal and external stresses combine to overwhelm couples and their families and threaten relationship breakdown.
- The chapter concludes with the couple therapist's perspective.

HAVE YOU READ?

Both therapists and couples contemplating therapy and/or separation may find support in:

Cullington, D. (2008). *Breaking Up Blues: A Guide to Survival and Growth*. London: Routledge.

Greene, G. (1951). *The End of the Affair*. London: Heinemann.

Jervis, S. (2011). *Relocation, Gender, and Emotion: a Psycho-Social Perspective on the Experiences of Military Wives*. London: Karnac.

Larkin, P. (1960). Talking in Bed. In: *The Whitsun Weddings* (1964). London: Faber & Faber.

Perel, E. (2017). *The State of Affairs: Rethinking Infidelity*. New York: Harper.

Wallerstein, J.S. & Kelly, J.B. (2004). *Surviving the Breakup*. New York: Basic Books.

REFERENCES

Balfour, A., Morgan, M., & Vincent, C. (2012). *How Couple Relationships Shape Our World*. London: Karnac.

Bates, L., Hoeger, K., Stoneman, M-.J., & Whitaker, A. (2021). *Domestic Homicides and Suspected Victim Suicides during the Covid-19 Pandemic 2020–2021*. London: Home Office. Retrieved 12.03.2024 from: https://assets.publishing.service.gov.uk/media/6124ef66d3bf7f63a90687ac/Domestic_homicides_and_suspected_victim_suicides_during_the_Covid-19_Pandemic_2020-2021.pdf.

Bion, W.R. (1962). *Learning from Experience*. London: Tavistock.

Burns, R. (1785). To a Louse. In: *The Complete Poems and Songs of Robert Burns* (2011). Glasgow: Waverley Books Ltd.

Cowan, C.P. & Cowan, C.A. (2000). *When Partners Become Parents: The Big Life Change for Couples*. Mahwah, NJ: Lawrence Erlbaum.

Dicks, H.V. (1967). *Marital Tensions*. London: Tavistock.

Donne, J. (1624). *Meditation 17: Devotions Upon Emergent Occasions* (repub. 2015). Cambridge: Cambridge University Press.

Galdiolo, S., Culot, S., Delannoy, P., Mauroy, A., Laforgue, F., & Gaugue, J. (2022). Harmful Stress-Related Couple Processes during the COVID-19 Pandemic and Lockdown. *Frontiers in Psychology*, 13. https://doi.org/10.3389/fpsyg.2022.819874.

Harrison, J. (2022). *Five Arguments All Couples (Need To) Have*. London: Profile Books.

Hewison, D., Clulow, C., & Drake, H. (2014). *Couple Therapy for Depression*. Oxford: Oxford University Press.

Kipling, R. (2020). *The Best of Rudyard Kipling*. Redditch, Worcestershire: Read Books Ltd.

Office for National Statistics, Census (2021). *Divorces in England and Wales*. Retrieved 15.03.2024 from: https://www.ons.gov.uk/peoplepopulationandcommunity/birthsdeathsandmarriages/divorce/bulletins/divorcesinenglandandwales/2022.

Shakespeare, W. (1962). *Hamlet.* In: *The Complete Works of William Shakespeare.* London, New York: Oxford University Press.

Strober, M. & Davisson, A., (2023). *Money and Love: An Intelligent Roadmap for Life's Biggest Decisions.* San Francisco: Harper One.

Usher, K., Bhullar, N., Durkin, J., Gyamfi, N., & Jackson, D. (2020). Family Violence and COVID-19: Increased Vulnerability and Reduced Options for Support. *International Journal of Mental Health Nursing,* 29(4), 549–552.

4

WHAT IS COUPLE THERAPY?

INTRODUCTION

This chapter describes couple therapy from a number of perspectives. It is seen first in its historical context, where its early story in the UK is used to provide an example of the influence of social factors in the development of couple therapy as a profession. The perspectives of how 'therapy' is perceived nowadays, and how 'counselling' and 'psychotherapy' are defined provide further contexts, along with the aims of the therapy and therapists. The chapter discusses what characterises therapists, and why they are predominantly female, before offering a comparison of couple and sex therapy, and a rationale for using the term couple therapy. The importance of couple therapists' awareness of diversity, together with their experience of personal therapy are emphasised. The final section suggests and addresses some questions that couples seeking therapy might ask, including what might be expected when making a contract.

A BRIEF HISTORY OF COUPLE THERAPY

Therapy specifically directed at the needs of troubled couples began to be developed in both the US and the UK during the 1930s. In the aftermath of World War One and the Great Depression, considerable social upheaval and change led to concerns that the increase in divorce and family breakdown would affect social cohesion. What emerged as a result in the UK provides one example of how societal anxiety grew into a movement, which in turn

DOI: 10.4324/9781003313403-4

gave rise to a new profession. Other nations have their own stories.

In the UK, 'marital counselling' was initially offered by clergy (notably, Herbert Gray), social workers, and doctors as an adjunct to their primary roles. In 1938, Gray founded the Marriage Guidance Council (MGC), now Relate. In its early days, this compassionate, although socially conservative, organisation reflected some of the wider society's worries about family disintegration and social disorder, and the possibility of links between public heath, sickness, and lax moral codes; in that connection, the periodical, *Marriage Hygiene*, was published between 1934–1947. Motivation is always hard to establish retrospectively, but it may be that the early impetus behind developing couple therapy was a strong desire to restore social conformity, rather than to enable couples to realise their relationship's emotional potential. In 1948, Enid Balint and Lily Pincus, both psychoanalytically trained social workers, founded the Family Discussion Bureau (later Tavistock Relationships), which also developed services for couples (Balfour, 2021).

Couples' and families' fortunes are inter-dependent, their health and wellbeing closely intertwined. Hence, it is paradoxical that although some therapeutic services to support them have been developed collaboratively, others have also been rivalrous, setting up different couple and family therapy training institutions informed by different theoretical approaches. Considerable energy has been funnelled into creating separate professional identities, as for example, expressing a divide between psychodynamic-psychoanalytic and systemic ways of thinking. Gurman and Fraenkel (2002) summarise this history.

Despite continuing concerns about couples' and families' distress, it took several decades for counselling and therapy for couples to be recognised as having parity with other mental health services. It is significant that, initially, those who joined and were trained by MGC and its sister organisations in the UK practised as volunteers, or for little pay. This meant that, unless working with couples was part of a primary working role in health or social services, couple therapy was practised charitably, rather than professionally.

Nowadays, there is increasing professional recognition of couple therapists and for the therapy itself. Nevertheless, services are not generally offered within the UK's National Health Service (NHS), but are available privately from voluntary organisations or private practitioners. It is a measure of the continuing social concern to address pain and distress felt at the heart of families that UK organisations like Relate and Tavistock Relationships continue today both as service and training providers. (See Appendix 2).

IT'S TIME TO TALK ABOUT 'THERAPY' – SOME DEFINITIONS

- *A therapeutic relationship* is a working relationship. The term 'therapy' is now widely used to cover a variety of experiences (including counselling and psychotherapy) involving purposeful talking about emotional or psychological difficulties.
- *Counselling and psychotherapy*: although they have much in common, counselling and psychotherapy might be thought of as being at either ends of a spectrum which shows the range of frequency of meetings and the intensity of the enquiry. Couple counselling, also known as 'relationship counselling', may take place on a weekly, fortnightly, or even monthly basis. But the depth of the psychological exploration undertaken in couple psychotherapy generally requires meetings to happen at least weekly, if not more frequently. Frequency is also discussed in Chapter 6.
- *The problem with 'therapy'*: as an umbrella term to include both counselling and psychotherapy, 'couple therapy' serves most purposes well. But the language used regarding 'therapy' itself is often problematic. For example, 'therapy' denotes 'treatment'. Some people choose to avoid any association with 'treatment' because it sounds medicalised. Further, even if the best doctor treats the *whole* person in their patient, the use of the word 'patient' (in psychotherapy and psychoanalysis) sometimes annoys therapy recipients because they do not consider themselves to be 'ill', and certainly not 'mentally ill'. They may prefer 'client' to 'patient' as it is less passive and

suggests a greater sense of agency. Therapy is also often described as a 'talking cure', but 'cure' suggests an outcome which no therapist can guarantee, and 'cure' is certainly too superficial to describe changes, however positive, in a relationship; its use is therefore not favoured in this book.

- *Couple or couples therapy?*: as explained in Chapter 1, 'couple therapy', a term which is more accepted in the UK, is used throughout this book in preference to 'couples therapy', which is more usual in the US. The singular 'couple' is preferred, making it then compatible with the singular use of 'child', 'adult', 'individual', and 'family' when referring to other forms of therapy.

- *But what of group therapy for couples?*: some therapy for couples does happen in groups, such as where several couples meet to discuss the difficulties in their relationship associated with parenting, depression, or alcohol or drug use. Group therapy may be favoured for reasons of economy and practicality. The efficacy of group work in particular settings is also seen in Cowan and Cowan's (2000) longitudinal study of partnering and parenting, and in Jones and Asen's (2002) and Hewison, Clulow, and Drake's (2014) studies of couples and depression.

- *Defining 'couple therapy'*: as can be seen in Chapter 6, 'couple therapy' may mean different things to different people. Generally speaking, however, it is best defined as a meeting or series of meetings in which one couple talks with a therapist about their relationship. In the early days of developing couple therapy, in the 1940s–1960s, it was common for partners in a couple each to meet separately with their own therapist before the four of them met together, or for a couple to meet in co-therapy with a pair of therapists (Dicks, 1967). Nowadays, however, it has become the norm for there to be one therapist. Because the prime focus of the therapy is not on each of the partners, but on the couple's *relationship* and the distress which their relationship causes them, it is important that the therapy remains *couple* focussed, so
  - it is not individual therapy done in pairs, i.e., when therapy predominantly concerning one partner is conducted in front of the other;

- it is not couple therapy by extension, i.e., when only one partner attends each session, except for occasional joint meetings.

By contrast, the focus of individual therapy is on an individual and their relationships, especially the relationship with themselves, while the focus of family therapy is on relationships in the family. Nevertheless, it is worth stressing that good couple therapy benefits greatly from the therapist's understanding of psychological distress in individuals, as well as couples, and their respective families. This enables a better understanding of what each partner brings to the relationship, and in effect, what they are wanting their partner to understand.

WHAT ARE THE BASIC AIMS OF COUPLE THERAPY?

Some inferences about couple therapy's aims may already be apparent from the above. They can be summarised as:

- *To create an environment in which it becomes safe for the couple to explore and discuss their relationship with an outsider*: the safety established enables a new three-way relationship to be built between couple and therapist, supported by trust and respect.
- *To enable couples to listen to and understand one another, and to work together to accept differences and disappointments so that they can discover what outcome will best suit them both*: the outcome may lead to staying together, or to separating.

WHAT ARE BASIC AIMS FOR THE THERAPIST?

The two basic aims above mean that the therapy must be anchored by the therapist as:

- Being focussed on the couple's relationship.
- Having no assumptions about what the best outcome is.
- Not taking sides.

COMPARING COUPLE AND SEX THERAPIES

Couple and sex therapies can be said to overlap in many ways:

- Most couples experiencing sexual difficulties also describe emotional relationship difficulties, and often emotional distress in couples affects their sexual relationship.
- Most couple therapists are willing to explore both sexual and relationship difficulties and their impact upon one another.
- Gurman and Fraenkel, however, describe the relationship between couple therapy and sex therapy as 'still unconsummated' (2002, p.238). Some practitioners have found it challenging to integrate fully the different kinds of therapy that are required. For example,
- Where the cause of the sexual difficulty is primarily physiological, the therapist may be required to offer more information, advice, and techniques. The sex therapist may guide a programme of instruction, with homework exercises for the couple to practise. In this way, therefore, it may be similar to a cognitive behavioural approach to general couple therapy. (See Chapter 6 and Campbell, 2023).

IS COUPLE THERAPY RELATED TO GROWTH?

Many therapists see their role in terms of supporting personal growth in their clients. Couple therapists often refer to developmental processes in couple relationships, in which the couple's relationship is supported so that it can grow in step with the partners' own needs to mature. Just as each partner has their own life-cycle journey, so too does their relationship. When growth is halted in one partner or in the couple together, they may seek therapy to unstick what has interrupted their progress. Chapter 9 also addresses this.

CAN DIFFERENT COUPLE THERAPIES BE SAID TO HAVE COMMON CHARACTERISTICS?

Gurman (2008) suggests that four features typify couple therapies:

1. *Timing*:
    - Understanding the importance of asking 'Why now?'
    - Intervening very early on in the therapy rather than spending time on assessment.

- Giving less time to considering the ending of couple therapy compared with that given in individual therapy.
2. *Clear setting of the focus*:
   - Choosing to focus on the 'presenting problems' rather than couples' habitual ways of interacting.
3. *Couple therapists are 'eclectic'*:
   - Reflecting a variety of approaches, they are generally open to both the 'inner' and the 'outer' person in their clients as well as to offering homework.
4. *The therapist-couple relationship is not as significant as in individual therapy*:
   - The relative brevity of the therapy means that the relationship developed with the therapist, sometimes known as the '**transference**', is not as intense.
   - The principal healing happens in the couple's relationship.

How well do Gurman's suggested features describe the couple therapies you as reader may have observed? They may give an accurate general picture of brief therapies and those using cognitive-behavioural or systemic methods, but are not true of the reflective approaches of psychodynamic–psychoanalytic therapists, as described in Chapters 6, 7, and 8.

WHO ARE THE THERAPISTS?

Because the relationship with the particular therapist is so important in couple therapy, questions about their identity become very significant. Couple therapists come from a variety of backgrounds in terms of both life experience and learning. For most, their training as couple therapists will have followed a training in individual counselling or psychotherapy, with perhaps a previous qualification as a psychologist or social worker.

Mind the Gender Gap

World-wide, about two thirds of therapists are women, greatly outnumbering men. Explanations for this gender imbalance vary; there are a number of probable causes, of psychological, social, historic, and economic origin.

The difficulty with speaking openly about emotions may disproportionately affect men, as both users and providers of therapy. From childhood, girls and women appear generally less inhibited than boys and men about disclosing their feelings. The pain of rejection may be felt as keenly, but men are more likely to have learned that it is important not to reveal vulnerability – e.g., 'Big boys don't cry!' Rather than do so, which may feel catastrophic, they may be more inclined to let their angry behaviour express their difficulties. While women report more depression, suicide rates are much higher in men. The difference with regard to men may be explained by:

- *As users of therapy*, men's reluctance to be seen as vulnerable may account for their difficulties in seeking individual psychological help, and extend to couples' inhibitions about receiving couple therapy.
- *As therapy providers*, men's relative reluctance to practise may also stem from cultural associations of masculinity with avoidance of vulnerability. Practising therapy means continual exposure to one's own and others' experiences of rejection, as well as of failure to respond under stress. This further justifies the requirement that professionally trained therapists should receive personal therapy. Its aim is to enable them to listen more effectively to their client(s), rather than to themselves. Knowing that a therapist is able to listen to distress without being overwhelmed themselves, or needing to compare it with their own experience, is enormously important. Personal therapy also ought to address male therapists' thinking about their own and other men's vulnerability.

'FEMINIZATION' OF THERAPY?

The gender gap is itself a source of debate and disquiet regarding the 'feminization' of the profession (Ostertag & McNamara, 1991). There are no intrinsic reasons to suggest that women are naturally more empathic than men, but there may be transference reasons, or pre-conceived assumptions, as to why some people in distress turn for a listening ear to one gender rather than another. Whatever gendered reasons have historically prevailed, these cultural norms have become economically cemented. In consequence:

- Women outnumber men in caring professions, reflecting the lower pay awarded.
- Women have identified more readily with the 'given' role of 'home-maker'.
- Most services for couples initially came from charities (e.g., MGC), attracting more women than men for reasons of availability and low remuneration.
- Counselling and psychotherapy for individuals were developed more from psychology than from medicine and psychiatry.
- Medicine and psychiatry initially promoted male applicants over female. Non-medical applicants were originally barred from training as psychoanalysts.
- During the 20th century, psychology recruited more women than men, who were drawn to better paid roles in medicine and psychiatry.

AND MIND THE DIVERSITY GAP

What can couples expect from therapists in terms of attitudes to diversity? Most agencies have policies regarding non-discriminatory practice, and reputable training courses leading to registration also address this. Not all couple therapists are registered, but enquiring couples are entitled to ask whether a therapist has considered, or better still has had training to explore, their assumptions about GSRD (see Chapter 2). These issues are not at all new, but renewed social awareness of them has encouraged therapists to be open, both to their own underlying prejudices, and to the impact of chronically experienced discrimination, or 'weathering', experienced by couples who are considered to be in a minority (Davids, 2011; McCann, 2022). Additionally, there are concerns about the under-representation in therapeutic services of black and ethnic minorities in both the UK and the US, despite the fact that people from these minority ethnic groups experience greater challenges to their mental health (APA, 2022).

USEFUL QUESTIONS TO ASK

Before embarking on couple therapy couples may want to know answers to the questions covered below.

How Long Does it Take?

The length of each meeting, or session, may vary according to the therapist (or any agency policy), ranging from 50–60 minutes to 90 minutes.

The length and number of meetings will depend partly on:

- What the couple wants;
- If the therapist works for an agency, what limitations it sets;
- The therapist's theoretical approach;
- What emerges from a consultation.

Consultation

Generally speaking, couples might expect their therapy to be preceded by an initial consultation with the therapist, sometimes comprising of between one and three meetings. Its purpose is to explore what the couple is looking for and to assess whether further couple therapy meetings are required or recommended. Chapter 9 addresses this further. For some couples, the consultation is enough; it either serves as a brief therapy, or proves that therapy is not what is wanted just now. For those deciding to continue, the agreement then made with the therapist takes account of whether the therapy is to be time-limited, or allowed to run its own course, perhaps to become long-term.

Compared with individual therapy, some consider couple therapy to be characteristically brief, (Gurman, Lebow, & Snyder, 2015). The length of therapy offered will be dictated partly by cost, and partly by the theory underpinning the method used. Some agencies, constrained by their funding and waiting lists, limit the number to between twelve and twenty sessions. Otherwise, agencies and private practitioners opt to offer a length of contract that fits their philosophy. Broadly then:

- Brief or short-term therapy particularly suits methods based on action, e.g., cognitive-behavioural approaches.
- Longer-term or 'time-unlimited' therapy suits approaches based on reflection, e.g., psychodynamic-psychoanalytic. Chapter 6 discusses this further.

Is a Referral Necessary?

Although some couples are referred by their GP, or as part of the therapy their children or family is receiving, usually couples, or one partner of a couple, self-refer.

How to Locate a Reputable Therapist?

Often, a particular therapist or agency is recommended by friends or other family members. Although there is currently no require-ment in the UK that couple therapists are qualified or registered to practise a brief search online will help to identify professional bodies and directories (Appendix 2 has useful links.) These organ-isations carefully monitor and keep updated registers of qualified therapists to assist the public in locating therapists who are geo-graphically accessible or who work online.

Therapists also often publish personal websites with informa-tion about qualifications, experience, fees, contact details, as well as the theoretical framework they use.

For the reasons stated above, it is advisable to be wary of agen-cies or therapists who suggest they can offer a 'cure' or answers to every problem.

Further enquiries may be needed to establish:

1. *How are fees negotiated?* Is a charge or donation expected? Can the rate and frequency of payment be negotiated? What hap-pens if an appointment is cancelled, or during holidays?

   Some therapists and agencies do not charge for an initial meeting, regarding this as an occasion for 'talks about talks' – to discuss how and whether to meet further.

2. *Do people have couple therapy at the same time as individual therapy?* Sometimes individual therapists recommend their client, and partner, also seek couple therapy. Ideally, the therapists and

clients concerned should confer about whether the respective therapists should make contact and what information can be shared.

3. *Is anything required before meeting?* Preparation for meeting is also discussed in Chapter 9. Some therapists suggest that couples write a summary, either together or separately, in advance of the first appointment, setting out what has prompted them to come and what they hope to gain from meeting.

4. *What should a couple look for in a therapist?* As well as details about registration and qualification, couples may want to enquire about the following before meeting a therapist:

   • What theoretical approach is used? Is homework given or expected? Does the therapist use questionnaires/reviews?
   • Is the meeting place a private space? Is there a waiting area if arriving early or separately? Is it acceptable to bring a baby/small child?
   • What languages are offered?

   Whether or not a couple and their therapist are compatible may not be apparent until they meet, or even until after two or three meetings. It might then be evident whether they:

   • Practise in a non-discriminatory way.
   • Are business-like, without being impersonal.
   • Respect confidentiality.
   • Are punctual and good time-keepers.
   • Have 'house-rules; e.g., regarding using phones, bringing coffee, contact outside sessions.

5. *Is it acceptable to try out several different therapists?* Couples who are searching for a good 'match' with a therapist may, of course, wish to try different approaches before committing themselves to what, after all, is an important step to take. Partners may not share the same degree of confidence in the therapist, or level of comfort with the approach. Or they may feel that they will get a better deal by shopping around. For the therapists concerned, this can disconcertingly feel like speed dating. If it happens repeatedly, a therapist should bring it to supervision. It may reveal couples' ambivalence, but perhaps it also tells the therapist that there is something to address about how they are presenting their service to couples.

Making a Contract

This is also discussed in Chapter 9. Here, it is worth noting that the questions listed above reflect couples' needs for assurance about how they will be received, and that their needs for respect, privacy, and security will be met. A shared understanding and agreement about this is an essential basis for the work. Contracts, either in the form of a verbal understanding, or a written document, describe terms for meeting and any arrangements to be followed should there be any need to re-negotiate. Most agencies prefer a written document.

The contract is seen by some as a '**secure base**'. Chapter 8 discusses John Bowlby's concept of a 'secure base'. As an agreed basis for therapy, a contract can be considered as part of that base. It provides a stable grounding for both couple and therapist during what may prove a disturbing time. At the same time, an opportunity to review and re-negotiate presents a good model for reconsidering and adapting to changing needs. If the therapist does not keep to the contract and fails to review and/or to adequately explain their reasons for this, this is an indicator of their reliability. If the couple finds it necessary continually to question and review the contract, this might communicate something important about how they see the place of agreements within their relationship.

Contract making therefore plays an especially significant role for couples who come to therapy with ambivalence, or even dread, rather than hope. Much of this important groundwork is undertaken during the first phase of the therapy, and described at greater length in Chapter 9.

LET US ASK OURSELVES ...

- As a therapist, what 'rules' would I be entitled to set out? And how would I explain or enforce them?
- If I put myself in the couple's shoes, what impression, positive or negative, would they have of me, as therapist, whether from my website or from my consulting room, about the therapy I offer?

CHAPTER SUMMARY

- This chapter addresses the various meanings of 'therapy' and the way in which it is understood. This is done through a brief history of couple therapy, a short discussion of what is

generally meant by 'therapy', and definitions of counselling and psychotherapy.
- Couple therapy is then considered from several perspectives, including its aims, what characterises therapists, and why they are predominantly female.
- A comparison with sex therapy is given.
- The importance of couple therapists' awareness of diversity, along with their experience of personal therapy is emphasised.
- A final section suggests and addresses some questions that couples seeking therapy might ask, including what might be expected from a contract.

HAVE YOU READ?

Abse, S. (2022). *Tell Me the Truth About Love: 13 Tales from the Therapist's Couch*. London: Ebury Press.

HAVE YOU SEEN?

Many professions feel challenged by the potential for AI to take over. The following film and film commentary explore this possibility:

Jonze, S. (dir.) (2013). *her*. Warner Bros.
Thompson, K. (2015). Review of *her*. *Couple and Family Psychoanalysis*, 5(1), 1107–1111.

REFERENCES

American Psychological Association (APA) (2022). Demographics of U.S. Psychology Workforce. Retrieved 16.06.23 from: https://www.apa.org/workforce/data-tools/demographics.

Balfour, A. (2021). A Brief History of Tavistock Relationships. In: M. Waddell & S. Kraemer (eds.) *The Tavistock Century: 2020 Vision* (pp.175–182). Bicester: Phoenix.

Campbell, C. (2023). *Sex Therapy: The Basics*. London: Routledge.

Cowan, C.P. & Cowan, C.A. (2000). *When Partners Become Parents: The Big Life Change For Couples*. Mahwah, NJ: Lawrence Erlbaum.

Davids, M.F. (2011). *Internal Racism*. London: Bloomsbury.

Dicks, H. (1967). *Marital Tensions*. London: Tavistock.

Gurman, A.S. (ed.) (2008). *Clinical Handbook of Couple Therapy*. New York and London: The Guilford Press.

Gurman, A.S. & Fraenkel, P. (2002). The History of Couple Therapy: A Millennial Review. *Family Process*, 41(2), 199–259.

Gurman, A.S., Lebow, J.L., & Snyder, D.K. (eds.) (2015). *Clinical Handbook of Couple Therapy* (5th ed.). New York and London: The Guilford Press.

Hewison, D., Clulow, C., & Drake, H. (2014). *Couple Therapy for Depression*. Oxford: Oxford University Press.

Jones, E. & Asen, E. (2000). *Systemic Couple Therapy and Depression*. London: Karnac.

McCann, D. (2022). *Same-Sex Couples and Other Identities*. London: Routledge.

Ostertag, P.A. & McNamara, J.R. (1991). 'Feminization' of Psychology: The Changing Sex Ratio and Its Implications for the Profession. *Psychology of Women Quarterly*, 15(3), 349–369.

WHAT BASIC SKILLS ARE REQUIRED?

INTRODUCTION

This chapter summarises the range of skills required when practising couple therapy. These include the basic skills nowadays expected of anyone working as an individual counsellor or psychotherapist as well as those that are specifically required when meeting with couples. Space limits preclude more than an introductory summary, but the reader is recommended to apply the information summarised here to the description of therapies in other closely linked chapters, as listed at the end of this chapter. Beginning with definitions of some commonly used terms, the chapter aims to show how the skills used when practising couple therapy provide the 'nuts and bolts' of the work, and that the acquisition of skills is not confined to one period of training, but becomes a natural companion on the therapist's journey of continuing learning. While different approaches to couple therapy, as described more fully in Chapter 6, promote different ways of working, the basic skills they use are broadly similar. Notably, however, psychodynamic-psychoanalytic approaches differ in requiring awareness of unconscious communication; and briefer therapies, such as cognitive-behavioural therapy, rely on therapists' skills in managing directive programmes. The chapter concludes with a summary of its contents.

SOME PRELIMINARY DEFINITIONS

To clarify their use in the context of this chapter, definitions are offered for closely associated, commonly used words. They are:

- *Skill*: the ability, developed by the use of knowledge and experience, to do something well.

DOI: 10.4324/9781003313403-5

- *Competence*: the ability to do something well enough or to a required degree.
- *Competency/competencies*: abilities defined by professional organisations and training bodies to assess the adequacy of members' and/or trainees' skills.
- *Technique*: a way of doing something, e.g., an approach to applying a particular skill.
- *Intervention*: an action by the therapist with the aim of enabling a useful change.

THE IMPACT OF PROFESSIONALISATION

Talking therapies for all kinds of clients have, over the past 50 years, become increasingly established and professionalised.

- *Training*: training for trainees and qualified practitioners, with requirements to attend courses for continuing professional development (CPD), have become progressively more sophisticated. Training courses vary in depth but may take from one to three years to complete. Trainees should expect that skills practice will be taught in role-play sessions and/or through supervised case-work.

   All therapeutic work is, or should be, a learning process for therapists, as well as clients.
- *Competence*: many registration bodies compile lists of competencies which accredited courses use in assessment for qualification. There is also some skill in knowing the limits of one's competence, and when to seek supervision.
- *The normalisation of supervision*: professional registration usually stipulates the receipt of regular supervision to safeguard both therapist and client.

A STARTING POINT FOR PRACTISING COUPLE THERAPY

Most therapists now working with couples will have started their therapeutic practice by training in counselling or psychotherapy with individuals and/or families. This becomes the foundation for the skills particularly needed in couple therapy. As explained in Chapter 13, this learning pathway is currently adopted by many

training institutes. Commonly used foundational skills are summarised in the following sections.

BASIC COUNSELLING AND THERAPY SKILLS

Many therapists may trace their learning back to approaches
described or inspired by Gerard Egan in *The Skilled Helper* (1994).
First published in 1975, and now in a sixth edition, it set out a
three-stage approach: clarifying the client's current story, establishing the preferred changes, and helping the client to work out
how to proceed. Other useful guides are referenced below (Culley, 1990; Howard, 2017; Jacobs, 2010).

Carl Rogers (1902–1987) was also influential in proposing the
three key elements of person-centred therapy, i.e., unconditional
positive regard or acceptance, empathy, and congruence.

These approaches have helped to define the therapeutic relationship as a new, particular way of conducting a helping relationship. Listed below are six important activities which have been
identified as integral aspects of this relationship, and for which
therapists require training in order to practise effectively for their
clients' benefit. Essentially, a therapist uses skills in relating that
require

- awareness of others' needs, and
- a sense of timing.

Listed below are six activities integral to a therapeutic
relationship.

1. *Listening*: including to what is said, and not said, through body
   language and behaviour.
2. *Relating empathically*: showing a sincere desire to know and
   understand the other emotionally.
3. *Reflecting back*: showing that the therapist has heard and understood the client's verbal and emotional communication.
4. *Non-judgemental acceptance*: respecting the client as an equal,
   including respect for diversity.
5. *Open-ended questioning*: showing that the therapist makes no
   assumptions about a right or wrong answer.

6. *Managing boundaries*: responding to all parties' needs to feel safe within the limits and possibilities of the therapeutic relationship, safeguarding rights to confidentiality and privacy; also thought of as the '**therapeutic frame**'.

BASIC COUPLE THERAPY SKILLS

Because couple therapy generally involves three people, the skills required can straightforwardly be thought of as specific extensions of those required in individual therapy. We must remember, however, that adding a third person introduces extra dimensions of complexity, so the couple therapist needs to use a different perspective. Each of the six processes of individual therapy identified above is therefore reviewed in relation to how they are affected by their use in a three-way relationship.

1. *Listening in a threesome*
   - *The client is now the couple's relationship*: the cartoonist, Mel Calman (1931–1994) once caricatured couple therapy, amusingly picturing a therapist and two people in bunk beds. But if this really expresses what couple therapy feels like, the thought of having to relate to two people on physically very separate levels is quite disturbing. With apologies for killing the joke, a more accurate image would have the therapist relating to two people, still expressing their separateness, but on the same level – as if in twin beds. Although there is a threesome, the focus of the therapy is placed on the couple's relationship in which they are both joined and separated. The therapist's skill thus lies in finding the links between the couple, as well as where those links are fragile or broken.

     The therapist's skill also lies in continually listening for what is being communicated by the partners, together and separately, about the couple's relationship. In psychodynamic-psychoanalytic couple therapy this is sometimes referred to as 'thinking couple' or having a '**couple state of mind**' (Morgan, 2018).
   - *Creating spaces for all to talk and listen*: this means being firm and fair. When relating to two or more people, in any

therapy setting, the therapist, as host, carries a role of either facilitating or organising the conversation, so that both partners can speak and listen to one another, and both feel heard by the therapist. The therapist consciously divides their attention between each partner, seeking, however tempting it may be, not to favour one more than the other. Asserting proper authority over turn-taking requires therapists' confidence, tact, and skill.

- *Listening to and managing conflict*: conflict has multiple dimensions. Couple therapists should expect to witness many distressing disagreements, which are sometimes aggressive and abusive. Open quarrelling may be informative and therefore constructive, provided that the therapist can intervene while a couple is still able to step back to reflect on the meaning of their differences. Upsetting sessions may allow for a better understanding of the couple's relating at home or enable a partner to express something they were previously unable to explain. Potentially too, they may lead to partners learning new ways of accepting each other's feelings and to making peace. But repeated angry quarrelling in sessions can be used to distract from addressing difficult issues, such as acknowledging shared grief or guilt.

  The therapist's skill lies in not taking sides, thinking about the meaning of the anger, and, when appropriate, intervening to call a halt in order to reflect on what the fight is expressing. Taking stock in this way is also crucial when there are indications of risk to either partner or to children at home.

- *Listening empathically in a threesome – bridging listening with empathy*: perceiving and understanding '**transference**' and '**countertransference**' are abilities that bridge listening and relating empathically. Perhaps most readily understood as non-verbal communications of feelings or states of mind, identifying transference and countertransference is considered fundamental to psychodynamic-psychoanalytic therapies, and is illustrated in examples given in Chapters 7, 9, and 10. Transference and countertransference experiences express otherwise unspoken (often unconscious) aspects of relationships: the relationship between the couple, the relationship between the therapist and the couple, and/or the relationship between the therapist and each partner.

The therapist's ability to receive these communications depends partly on their sensitivity, or emotional intelligence, and partly on their experience either as a therapist or in their own personal therapy. Experienced therapists learn to recognise feelings which appear to be 'foreign' and arrive unexpectedly, such as unaccountable sensations of dread, sleepiness, or grief.

2. *Relating empathically*
   - *Containing a couple's pain and complexities*: as is described in several chapters, the therapist is called upon to act as a '**container**', a concept used in psychodynamic-psychoanalytic therapies. We might picture a scenario in which all that is overwhelming the couple, and which has become too much to bear, 'spills' out in the therapy. Perhaps their pain feels greater because no-one else has been able or willing to hear it. If the therapy is to be effective, the therapist needs to be able to show not only willingness to hear and think about the couple's grief and perhaps grievance without dismissing it, but also that they can reflect back to the couple's ways of thinking about what is so distressing, which may help to make it more bearable. Thinking in the powerful presence of two people who are beside themselves with all that has divided them requires the therapist to feel empathically while also retaining their own sense of self. This is akin to the '**meta position**' described in Chapter 12.

3. *Reflecting back*
   - *Timing and wording an interpretation:* as is also explained and illustrated by an example in Chapter 7, an '**interpretation**' is a statement by a therapist aimed at sharing with the client/couple the therapist's understanding of what has been said or has happened. As an intervention, it is an example of a technique that some approaches, for example behavioural therapies, consider unnecessary. It is, however, a key feature of psychodynamic-psychoanalytic approaches.

The therapist's skill is involved in deciding when and how to phrase the interpretation and, crucially, what use – if any – the couple makes of it. A poorly worded or premature interpretation will, at best, fall on deaf ears; at worst, it will be considered evidence of insensitivity. Noting how the therapist's perception is received by each partner, and by them as a couple, requires a particular aptitude and experience on the part of the therapist. When it works well, it becomes the basis for further productive exploration of issues that are difficult. When it 'falls on stony ground', the therapist's skill lies in knowing how and whether to use that experience of a missed communication.

4. *Non-judgemental acceptance*
   - *Respecting diversity (GSRD) and clients' preferred outcomes*: while this is now covered in most reputable training courses, the new millennium brought with it a sea-change in social attitudes of what is desirable and acceptable. Therapists thus need insight with which to challenge their own beliefs and sense of identity, and seek out any unexplored prejudices and assumptions which are out of place in their therapeutic practice.

5. *Open-ended questioning*
   - *Modelling a freedom to explore*: couple therapy is predicated on offering a resource couples can use to find ways of managing difficulties which they might struggle to find on their own. The therapist is allotted the role of someone who does not necessarily know, but wants to be curious, as compared with someone who does not know and does not want to know. Circular questioning, as in systemic therapies (Chapter 6), is used as a way of opening up the dynamic in the therapy room as well as encouraging the understanding of others' thoughts and feelings. Both this, and taking authority for the right to be curious (Chapter 1), are techniques that express and model an important and liberating way of being.

6. *Managing boundaries*
   - *Maintaining the 'therapeutic frame'*: the notion of a frame that holds the therapeutic relationship between therapist and clients within boundaries, which are defined by its

purposes, is more fully discussed in Chapters 9 and 10. Principally used in relation to psychoanalytic therapies, it is a metaphorical concept, describing the extent and limits of the understanding between the therapist and the client. The therapist's task is to hold this frame in mind in order to safeguard the therapy and the client. In their training, therapists are encouraged into good habits of time-keeping in sessions and thinking reflectively after sessions. Observing the therapeutic frame further supports maintaining the focus on the client couple. It encourages the therapist to be discreet about their own circumstances, however tempting it is to identify with the experiences the couple describe, or to risk appearing to be withholding when asked personal questions.

- But not all couple therapists see boundaries in the same way, as noted below.

SOME NOTABLE DIFFERENCES

Although all couple therapy approaches employ skills used in the basic activities listed above, different theoretical approaches have required their respective followers to develop particular techniques, as Chapters 6, 7, and 8 show. Here, however, it may be helpful to highlight some differences of approach which prioritise different techniques and skills from therapists. For example, skills in management and teaching are required when using programmes devised for therapy that is brief or time-limited, and goal-directed; clients are led by the therapist through a tailored course of therapy, sometimes with 'homework'.

Therapists are therefore in debate over what approach is most helpful and what skills are needed. In summary, the areas of contention are:

- Boundary management: self-disclosure to demonstrate authenticity versus maintaining the focus on clients' relationships.
- Advice giving versus non-directive approaches.
- Advice giving versus information giving.
- Teaching versus allowing clients' self-discovery.

WHAT THEN ARE INDISPENSABLE SKILLS?

- *Holding consistently to an approach* which the therapist believes in and can support as being appropriate to each couple's particular needs.
- *Knowing one's limitations*: some therapists are deterred from practising couple therapy by fear that couples' mutual anger will be unmanageable and become even physically, as well as verbally expressed. Witnessing both open conflict and covert emotional abuse is always distressing. Respect should always be given for recognition of the limits of tolerance and capabilities. For therapists who find anxiety about conflict disabling, it is wise, as well as ethical, not to practise couple therapy.
- *Being honest*: saying 'I don't know'. Not knowing is a painful state of mind, but therapists need to be able to own it, not least because it models the courage to wait to find a way forward.
- *Recognising overload*: couples often come to therapy because they are overwhelmed. If the therapist feels unable to contain them, either due to the number of their clients, or by events in their own lives, it is essential that they recognise the signals and seek the support of supervision. This means monitoring tolerance and stress levels. Apart from burnout in the therapist, the risks are otherwise that unconscious barriers are put up against conflict and pain, and issues, such as levels of aggression between a couple, or that a couple's circumstances chime with difficulties in their own life, are overlooked.
- *Safe-guarding the therapy setting*: both the couple and the therapist have to feel safe and secure for any useful work to occur. Some agencies have policies that couples with a history of violence are not seen together, out of a concern that the abused partner is not put at further risk.
- *Readily challenging oneself*: couple therapy can be such a 'busy' experience, it is salutary to be reminded not to be so swept along by the detail of the story that the need for continual self-questioning remains overlooked. Examples of challenging questions therapists can ask themselves are: 'What is not being said?', 'What am I not seeing?', and 'Am I feeling too comfortable with this couple?'

CONCLUSION

Some aspects of working as a couple therapist feature in both individual and couple therapy, but meeting a couple requires that the therapist adds extra dimensions to their thinking. Regarding the care that the couple and their family need at the point of seeking help, the most important factors are time, commitment to the work, an open mind, and a capacity to hear their pain. Then they need their therapist to listen and reflect back to them the picture they are portraying of their relationship so that they can either change it or, if they choose, let it go.

Noting that couple therapists must be ready to be receptive to *whatever* sorrows any new couple chooses to bring, how might therapists prepare themselves? It can seem a tall order, but the couple needs their therapist to be calm and un-shockable; and even though there may be no immediate 'answers', being wary and tentative is not a welcome response. Chapter 13 addresses in more detail the levels of training that enable a therapist to feel grounded in the work at the level at which they choose to practise. In this, it is wise to seek out a training programme in which to explore and rehearse the skills needed before they are required by the qualified therapist.

A POST-SCRIPT: LINKS WITH OTHER CHAPTERS

The skills summarised above in this chapter are applications of the many aspects of couple therapy which are amplified in other chapters as follows:

- Chapter 4, 'What is couple therapy?' distinguishes between therapy for individuals and therapy designed for couples.
- Chapter 6, 'Different kinds of couple therapy' shows that different approaches require particular skills related to their approach.
- Chapter 7, 'What is psychodynamic–psychoanalytic couple therapy?', and Chapter 8, 'Further couple therapies linked to psychoanalysis', spell out the specific techniques required in psychodynamic–psychoanalytic therapies.

- Chapter 9, 'First meetings with a couple,' and Chapter 10, 'Ongoing meetings and challenges in couple therapy' consider the skills required in assessment and in maintaining the therapeutic relationship.
- Chapter 12, which argues for the importance of supervision, shows how it underpins the therapist's skills.
- Chapter 11 and Chapter 13, in exploring endings, new beginnings, and continuing learning, emphasise the importance of review and openness to theoretical learning and practice skills.

LET US ASK OURSELVES ...

- What skill or technique seems most challenging and how would one know it is practised well enough?
- Can things be put right in therapy if they are unskilfully mismanaged?

CHAPTER SUMMARY

- The range of skills required in couple therapy is summarised. They include the basic skills of those working as an individual therapist *plus* those that are specifically drawn on in couple therapy.
- Definitions of some commonly used terms are set out to clarify their meaning in the context of the chapter, before listing the chief features of the therapeutic process and setting out the skills that are associated with them in couple therapy.
- Some skills specifically associated with awareness of unconscious communication are explained.
- A final post-script listing chapters that develop some of the issues described is offered as a guide.

HAVE YOU READ?

Bubenzer, D.L. & West, J.D. (1993). *Counselling Couples*. London: Sage.

Novakovic, A. & Reid, M. (eds.) (2018). *Couple Stories*. Abingdon: Routledge.

HAVE YOU SEEN?

Baumbach, N. (dir.) (2019). *Marriage Story*. Borehamwood, Herts: Heyday Films Ltd. And for commentary on the film, see:

Nyberg, V. (2021). Review of *Marriage Story*. *Couple and Family Psychoanalysis*, 11(1), 94–98.

REFERENCES

Calman, M. (1980). *But It's My Turn To Leave You*. London: Mandarin.

Culley, S. (1990). *Integrative Counselling Skills*. Los Angeles, London: Sage.

Egan, G. (1994). *The Skilled Helper*. New York: Brooks Cole Publishing Company.

Howard, S. (2017). *Skills in Psychodynamic Counselling and Psychotherapy* (2nd ed.). London: Sage.

Jacobs, M. (2010). *Psychodynamic Counselling in Action*. Los Angeles, London: Sage.

Morgan, M. (2018). *A Couple State of Mind*. London and New York: Routledge.

6

DIFFERENT KINDS OF COUPLE THERAPY

INTRODUCTION

Chapter 4 gave a general introduction to therapy with couples. This chapter picks up the baton to give more information about four main kinds of couple therapy, recognising that the scope of this book does not allow space for a comprehensive presentation of all of those available. The therapies chosen are behavioural, emotionally focussed, psychodynamic-psychoanalytic, and systemic, although a more detailed description of psychodynamic-psychoanalytic approaches is given in Chapters 7 and 8. The links between theories and therapy are discussed, together with criteria for making a choice of therapy, and the efficacy of research. The chapter concludes with a summary.

BACKGROUND: THE BIG PICTURE

Since its first development in the 1940s, couple therapy has proliferated, now taking many forms. Almost everyone has something to say about couples, whether their perspective is psychological, sociological, political, anthropological, or ethical, and all of these perspectives have contributed to the shaping of ideas about couples and how best to support them. If you are new to exploring therapy in general, some of the differences between the various types of couple therapy can be confusing. Perhaps it helps to draw a mental picture?

DOI: 10.4324/9781003313403-6

Picturing Different Therapies and the Relationships Between Them

In the process of its development, the practice of psychotherapy – including therapy and counselling – has branched out in several directions. Each type bears its own name, claiming its separate identity. To picture the whole range of therapies we might imagine a large building called 'The Department of Mental Health and Emotional Wellbeing'. On entering, we might seek out the floor marked 'Psychotherapies'. Ahead, a corridor leads to suites of rooms, each with name plates such as 'Cognitive-Behavioural', 'Psychodynamic', 'Systemic', 'Relational', 'Gestalt', 'Attachment', 'Psychoanalytic', and many more.

Each room is furnished in a particular style; there will be book cases – perhaps even small libraries – filled with books and journals by authors who have adopted that way of thinking; their portraits may even adorn the walls. The libraries will have different sections – child and adolescent, adult, couple, family, psychosexual – so you can look for the 'couple' section in each one. In the psychoanalytic library you will be able to look up what Freud said about the 'narcissism of small differences' (1930a).

Generally, there will be secluded spaces set aside for personal therapy or counselling, perhaps furnished as an office with tables and chairs, or a couch. There may be pot plants, and the walls might either be decorated with art works or be relatively bare. There will usually be a box of paper hankies and a jug of water.

Often, there will be doors off to adjoining rooms, so that the links between different ways of thinking can be more easily made and kept. Examples of this would be the links between cognitive and behavioural rooms, between cognitive and analytic, psychodynamic and psychoanalytic, and another between attachment and psychodynamic. As well as having doors leading off, the walls of the main rooms might often be permeable, allowing those who so choose to be aware of what is going on in discussions and teaching next door.

Visitors to these suites of rooms will come for different reasons – to try out the therapy, and/or to borrow the books, to stay a while and study, perhaps to make a career, or perhaps to dip into a variety of ways of thinking about life and relationships to see what suits or fits them best.

So Much in Common, But So Insistent on Differences

Couple therapy creates important new dynamic forces:

- A three-way relationship forms between therapy, theory, and the therapist.
- A two-way relationship is established between the couple and the therapist.

This relationship created by the couple and their therapist is recognised as the most significant factor in the success of the therapy, whichever kind of therapy couples choose.

Common features are:

- All couple therapies aim to alleviate the distress caused by relationship breakdown and its serious impact on couples, children, families, and the wider community.
- All therapies offer support through providing a relationship which models ways of managing stressful life events.

But different approaches are used:

- Each insists on using their own particular language to describe very similar emotional and relationship difficulties.
- They also differ in the methods and techniques they use.

Comparative Responses to Social Upheaval?

Political: all couple therapies emerged during the socially turbulent decades following World War One. All have attempted to address challenges posed by continual social change. Some have aimed to restore the status quo; others have recognised the need for adaptation and change.

Personal: it may be unsurprising that the relationship style a couple therapist offers is greatly influenced by their own belief systems and personality. Gurman (2008, p.16) has described three distinct roles taken by therapists: "the educator/coach, the perturbator, and the healer".

Would-be therapists are therefore faced with a number of decisions:

- Which of the three roles should I model?
- Which theory is going to fit best with my preferred style of working?
- How will the ways I manage closeness (intimacy) and separateness (objectivity) affect couples so they feel confident to explore matters about which they feel vulnerable?

These three questions show how closely therapies are linked with theories; indeed, therapies grew out of theories. But why have theories been so important?

THEORY: THE LOVE-CHILD OF UNCERTAINTY AND ANXIETY?

'Theory: an idea used to account for a situation or justify a course of action.'
(Oxford English Dictionary)

Human beings have been described as meaning-making, meaning-seeking creatures, reflecting their continual attempts to understand why things happen. That understanding is often crucial in recovery from trauma. Therapists meet with couples who may be traumatised, are often confused, and who struggle to settle differences. To understand what has happened, it seems rational to wonder whether the couple's experience fits recognisable patterns from which therapists have previously learned what responses might work best. Identifying patterns and their possible causes offer therapists and couples ways of feeling grounded when similar quandaries recur. Theories, with their hypotheses explaining causes and probable mitigations, may thus provide reassuring explanations, if not a welcome sense of certainty.

Uncertainty is universally troubling. The 20th century has been called 'the age of uncertainty', perhaps in response to the world's complexity and our struggles to make sense of it all. Theories that underlie all psychological therapies, including couple therapy, reflect two different ways of reacting to uncertainty. Many therapies include a mixture of both and can be presented as:

- *Reflection versus action*: anxious and disempowered about what to do next, we feel caught between reflection (stepping back to think about the problem), and action ('carrying on regardless'). Reflection allows time to take account of the effect of the past on the present, whereas action prompts taking a 'here and now' approach. Broadly speaking then, analytical theories value reflection on the underlying and *past* causes of relationship difficulties in order to discover how to manage them in the present; and behavioural theories, while seeking to explain what has gone awry, focus on what action should *now* be taken to change things for the better.

- *Working from the inside outwards versus working from the outside in*: Clulow (1985) describes the first as holding to the idea that inner, sometimes unconscious beliefs, are key in shaping and thus changing behaviours and relationships; the second route works to alter the environment (e.g., the family around a couple) in order to support the couple to adapt their relationship.

Here, then, are three clear differences of approach:

1. *Psychoanalytic and psychodynamic therapies* focus on long-standing and even unrecognised, because they are unconscious, sources of the couple's conflict.
2. *Behavioural and cognitive-behavioural therapies* seek more rational 'here and now' explanations of what has gone wrong and thus ways of correcting it.
3. *Systemic therapies* take account of circumstances in the couple's environment which may impact their abilities to adapt.

Contrasting these approaches in somewhat binary, either/or ways does not do justice to the range of therapies now available, but defines the scope for the whole couple therapy spectrum. The width of this spectrum may explain why, in fact, most couple therapists are eclectic, drawing on more than one, if not several, theoretical perspectives in their clinical practice. While this may lead to criticism from purists in different fields, bringing ideas together can also be thought of as a therapeutic way of reflecting the bringing together of two different people's understanding of a third unhappy party – their shared relationship. Indeed, the 21st century has seen the development of therapies that deliberately seek to bridge the gaps between approaches. One example is integrative couple therapy (ICT), for which therapists consciously combine a number of different approaches to meet specific difficulties (Gurman, 2008). Another example is seen in the combining of psychoanalytic therapy with mentalization techniques for couples who struggle to manage their anger in sessions.

THE IMPORTANCE OF INCLUSION

Before detailing the main therapies, it is appropriate to foreground more recent developments in couple therapies to include the concerns and welfare of couples who have previously experienced discrimination, and who have been side-lined, or overlooked.

- *Unconscious bias*: some continuing short-fall arises, not necessarily always as a result of deliberate discrimination, but because so much bias is unconscious and therefore more likely to be overlooked. An anti-discriminatory (and not merely a non-discriminatory) approach should be embedded, in a front and centre way, into teaching about couple therapy. It should be seen as a natural part of a couple therapist's non-judgmental value system, with the understanding that we are all subject to beliefs about others which, as therapists, we should continually review. An anti-discriminatory approach thus sits naturally alongside the understanding that each couple's experience is unique.
- *Feminist thinking*: this has highlighted the gendered expectations of women as partners, and flagged their greater vulnerability as victims of partner violence.
- *Multicultural perspectives*: it has become increasingly more important to take account of these perspectives in couples' lives to find ways of acknowledging the 'othering', the slights, and the emotional weathering experienced by couples who are Black, of mixed race, or of different ethnicities.
- *Gender and sexual diversity*: it is essential to hear and accept the experience of couples whose relationships reflect such diversity.

Publications that adequately address these issues appear continually to be running to catch up with the tide. Readers may, however, find encouragement to broaden their thinking from: British Psychoanalytic Council (2023); Charura & Lago (2021); Lago & Smith (2010); and McCann (2022).

THE MAIN COUPLE THERAPIES

As noted above, this book focusses on four types of couple therapy, each of which is based on a particular way of understanding personality and relationships:

- Behavioural;
- Emotionally focussed;
- Systemic;
- Psychodynamic-psychoanalytic.

Each is briefly defined and categorised under the following headings:

- Background (a brief history of the therapy);
- Principal features of this therapy grouped under 'Aims', 'Focus', and 'Therapist's Role';
- Further information (suggested further reading).

Readers are encouraged to spot parallel or similar features and the links between therapies. In the grand scheme of therapies, who found (or, more accurately, who first described) the ideas might be considered relatively unimportant. Moreover, parallel or challenging statements in response might better be heard as an ongoing conversation in the family of therapies to manage anxieties posed by continual social change.

BEHAVIOURAL COUPLE THERAPIES

BACKGROUND

From the 1970s onwards, various behavioural therapies, including behavioural marital therapy, cognitive behavioural couple therapy (CBCT), and integrative behavioural couple therapy

(IBCT), have been devised. Drawing on the principles of social learning, behaviour that is seen to be problematic can be changed by demonstrating better strategies; and thinking and beliefs that are negatively undermining can be examined and diffused. The practice of mindfulness and positive psychology may also be included.

PRINCIPAL FEATURES

Aims

- Overall aim: to enable couples to become their own therapist.
- The therapy aims to be short-term.
- Successful therapy depends on the couple and the therapist creating a good relationship.

Focus

- Emphasis is on the 'here and now' rather than problems from the past.
- Sessions are structured with goal-directed exercises tailored to the couple, including homework.
- Couples are taught how to identify recurring difficulties, e.g., anger management, with techniques to improve communication and build trust.

Therapist's Role

The role is linked with associated skills of listening, relating empathically, and reflecting back, as described in Chapter 5.
- Therapist takes a role as 'educator/coach' with the couple's active collaboration; their participation is essential.

Further Information

- Christensen, Doss, & Jacobson (2014) – IBCT-inspired book aimed at couples' self-help.
- Crowe & Ridley (2000).

EMOTIONALLY FOCUSSED THERAPY (EFT)

BACKGROUND

EFT has grown out of the work of Greenberg and Johnson (1988). The explicit inclusion of 'emotion' in the title signifies its potentially positive role in bringing about change, and not merely as a cause of couples' problems. EFT aims to help partners to reconsider their emotional interactions to strengthen relationship bonds. Its methods have lent it to being tested in research, with the result that EFT has established important links with the work of John Gottman (Gottman & Silver, 1999), attachment theory, and with systems theory.

PRINCIPAL FEATURES

Aims

- Establishes emotion as the chief player in relationships.
- Believes in human beings' fundamental capacities for growth.

Focus

- Focusses on *here and now* interactions *between* couples.
- Lends itself to short programmes of 8–20 meetings.

Therapist's Role

The following features are also linked with associated skills of listening, relating empathically and reflecting back, non-judgemental acceptance, open-ended questioning, and boundary management, as described in Chapter 5.

- Places the therapist as consultant to the couple rather than a coach, empathically acknowledging their experience rather than directing them to be different.
- Methodically charts nine steps in a process of change; change moves from identifying and de-escalating negative cycles of relating, through engaging the withdrawing partner, to replacing blame with recognition of underlying feelings.

Further Information

- Johnson (2019).

SYSTEMIC COUPLE THERAPY

Background

Systems theory was derived from Ludwig von Bertalanffy's observations that an understanding of individual parts of any system does not explain how they interact in the whole system. This idea was taken up in the 1950s by Murray Bowen and others to develop family therapy and later couple therapy, because they found the early focus by psychoanalysis on individuals inadequate.

Principal Features

The following list is relatively expanded in order to show the influence of systemic ideas on other forms of couple therapy with which there are many overlaps.

Aims

- Recognising subsystems and boundaries, e.g., there are three subsystems in families (couple, parents, and siblings), which may jostle to have their needs met so that boundaries between them get blurred, as when a parent's overly close (enmeshed) relationship with a child excludes the other parent/partner.
- Perceiving the family as multi-generational, i.e., relationship patterns are often repeated in successive generations. Discovering them can lead to a sense of relief and an opportunity to change course.

Focus

- Focus on here and now interactions between partners.
- Seeing causes as 'circular' (not linear), i.e., difficulties in relationships seen as resulting from several factors. Better to think about the problem 'in the round' than look for first causes.

- Mapping a couple's place in family's life cycle (see Chapter 8 for significance of the couple's place): couples can find themselves out of kilter with specific expectations newly laid on them, e.g., as parents of small children or carers for their parents.
- Registering partners' relative emotional growth and maturity of the couple relationship itself (see Chapter 8 on developmental dimensions). Ideally, partners' emotional growth is experienced in parallel allowing their relationship to be mutually satisfying.
- Appreciating the 'differentiation of self' in *both* the client and the therapist, i.e., the therapist recognises partners' progress in growth and separation from their parents, *and* the therapist retains a separate sense of themselves and so avoids over-identifying with couple.

Therapist's Role

These features can also readily be associated with listening and reflecting back skills described in Chapter 5.

- Taking in communication and meta-communication, i.e., listening to what is said and not said.
- Drawing a genogram with a couple to assist in assessment (see Chapter 9).
- Understanding homeostasis and morphogenesis, i.e., recognising the potential, after a crisis, for couples and families to alternate between reverting to type and changing.
- Using circular questioning to focus on the relationship, e.g., 'When you laughed just now, what do you think your partner was thinking?'
- Noting the frequency of **'triangulation'**: under stress, two people often seek support from a third, e.g., a mother whose partner has affairs makes their eldest daughter a confidante.

FURTHER INFORMATION

- Crawley & Grant (2008).
- Chew-Helbig (2023) – explores links between systems theory and Gestalt approaches.

PSYCHODYNAMIC-PSYCHOANALYTIC COUPLE THERAPY

Readers are directed to Chapter 7 to find a detailed description of this approach. Additional related applications – attachment theory, link theory, mentalization, and selfobject couple therapy – are summarised in Chapter 8. However, at this point it may be interesting to note that early forms of couple therapy, from the 1920s and 1930s, were probably most influenced by ideas that stemmed from psychoanalytic thinking. Moreover, couple therapies that followed have been thought of either as developments from psychoanalysis, or as reactions against it.

WHAT INFLUENCES THERAPISTS' CHOICE OF APPROACH?

THE POWER OF INDIVIDUALISM

It is useful to remember that couple therapies originated from earlier ideas about individual psychology and therapies. Ideas about couple relationships evolved and widened in the 20th century to include families, couples, and groups. Gradually, the therapies designed for families and couples have come to be recognised as valid in their own right. Nevertheless, in societies such as in the UK and USA, individualism continues to predominate and the broader perspective necessary for couple therapy can struggle for acceptance as being equally well-grounded and worthy of professional support.

SUBJECTIVITY VERSUS OBJECTIVITY?

The choice of which theory and method to follow will, however, most probably be dictated by the therapist's subjective beliefs, based on what feels most compatible with their own life experiences. Even if eclectic, most couple therapists will be inclined to be either more reflective or more directive. Their core beliefs about relationships will influence how best to react when faced with raw pain, deep disquiet, and uncertainties about the future. Jones and Asen (2000) note that experienced therapists are unlikely to follow a 'pure model' as, over time, their practice becomes personalised, reflecting the learning gained from experience. A theory that has been thought about, tried and tested, and which can be tested again in discussion with a supervisor, will provide an anchor and a way of continuing to think despite the storms in the therapy room.

THE SWAY OF FASHION

Theories about the best ways to address social distress and anxiety ebb and flow in waves. In the past forty years, postmodernism has expressed a widespread scepticism that there could be rational explanations (and thus theories) for everything. This way of viewing our search for meaning has supported the tendency in therapists to combine several different perspectives rather than following a single set of beliefs. Nevertheless, there are continuing vigorous debates about which theoretical approach is best. While the rivalry is sometimes destructively dismissive, there is also health in the conflict, just as there is health in couples who are able to assert and argue about their differences.

SEARCH FOR IDENTITY OR 'GROUP THINK'?

'Schools' of theories, further developed by academics, grow up around different ways of thinking. Theorists develop their own particular language. It asserts their separate identity, with the downside being that it can become jargon and alienating to outsiders. Often different terms are used to describe the same or similar phenomena. Nevertheless, being part of a particular school helps its followers to feel more secure. Thus, along with a sense of an identity, familiar theories provide therapists with ready 'go to' ways of understanding difficult issues, and a sense of authority because they are not alone. Theories are, or should be, dynamic – as if living – and continually tested by experience and developed to fit the changing world around the practitioner. Lewin (1952) famously observed: 'There is nothing more practical than a good theory'. This influence is seen in the take-home messages of the many self-help books produced today. Examples are:

- Abse (2022) describes the approach of a psychoanalytic couple therapist.

- Johnson (2008) sets out the EFT approach.
- Ludgate and Grubr (2018) offer exercises based on CBCT strategies.

WHICH THERAPIES WORK BEST?

Early research into which theories best informed the methods therapists found most useful was carried out in the form of clinical studies, such as those described by Dicks (1967). Gurman and Fraenkel (2002) have summarised the history and usefulness of research in this field. Research is important because it helps to demonstrate how the methods used measure up against the subjective judgements made about them. But research itself must always be evaluated sceptically, since not all therapies can be assessed using the same methods such as randomised controlled trials (RCT). (See Appendix 1 for more information on research).

Further questions arise:

- How is a successful outcome to be described?
- If a key component of a successful therapy is the relationship created between the therapist and the couple, what criteria are used to judge it?
- How can we be truly sure that the therapy offered is tailored to the couple's needs?

CONCLUSION

What lessons can be drawn? Many problems arise when trying to compare the efficacy of different therapies. The standard tests used by RCT for medical treatments of physiological problems are inappropriate, because psychological treatments vary so widely in their methods. Human beings are such complex creatures and themselves change over time, and couples receiving therapy are not to be pinned down like butterflies. Some services diligently monitor client satisfaction with systematic surveys using 'Clinical Outcomes in Routine Evaluation' (CORE). But this does not satisfactorily take account of several factors that are hard to measure. For example, couples may award scores because they are concerned not to appear 'difficult'. Or couples' scores may reflect short-term dissatisfaction with a therapy, while failing to register that after the therapy ended it nevertheless led to a happier resolution.

So what does success look like? The partners lived together 'happily ever after', or the partners separated and lived separately 'happily ever after'? Such outcomes can only be truly evaluated in long-term inclusive studies.

LET US ASK OURSELVES ...

- Since the scope of this chapter has had to be limited, what other therapies would you include?
- Which aspects of couple therapies do you most approve of and which are you most critical of?
- What criteria would you use to assess the success of a couple therapy?

CHAPTER SUMMARY

- The different methods, and their underlying theoretical perspectives, used by couple therapists are listed in terms of four principal methods: behavioural, EFT, systemic, and psychodynamic- psychoanalytic.
- With a focus on all (except psychodynamic-psychoanalytic, which is detailed in Chapters 7 and 8), each is described in terms of its background, principal ideas, and suggested further sources of information.
- The links between theories and therapy are discussed, together with criteria for making a choice of therapy, and the efficacy of research.

HAVE YOU READ?

Roth, A. & Fonagy, P. (2006). *What Works for Whom? A Critical Review of Psychotherapy Research*. New York: The Guilford Press.

Although focussing on therapy with individuals, this book helps to support readers' critical appraisal of therapies in general.

HAVE YOU SEEN?

Bergman, I. (dir.) (1973). *Scenes from a Marriage*. Sverige Radio.

REFERENCES

Abse, S. (2022). *Tell Me the Truth About Love: 13 Tales from Couple Therapy*. London: Ebury Press.

British Psychoanalytic Council (BPC) (2023). Bibliography on Gender, Sexuality and Relationship Diversity. Retrieved 8.03.2024 from: www.bpc.org.uk/?s=GSRD+Bibliogrpahy.

Charura, D. & Lago, C. (eds.) (2021). *Black Identities and White Therapies: Race, Respect and Diversity*. Monmouth: PCCS Books.

Chew-Helbig, N. (2023). How does Psychotherapy Work? General Systems Theory and Synchronization. *The Psychotherapist*. Retrieved 19.01.24 from: https://nikhelbig.at/how-does-psychotherapy-work-general-systems-theory-and-synchronization/.

Christensen, A. Doss, B.D., & Jacobson, N.S. (2014). *Reconcilable Differences: Rebuild Your Relationship by Rediscovering the Partner You Love – Without Losing Yourself* (2nd ed.). New York: The Guilford Press.

Clulow, C. (1985). *Marital Therapy: An Inside View*. Aberdeen: Aberdeen University Press.

Crawley, J. & Grant, J. (2008). *Couple Therapy*. Basingstoke and New York: Palgrave Macmillan.

Crowe, M. & Ridley, J. (2000). *Therapy with Couples: A Behavioural-Systems Approach to Couple Relationship and Sexual Problems* (2nd ed.). Oxford: Blackwell.

Dicks, H.V. (1967). *Marital Tensions*. London: Tavistock.

Freud, S. (1930a). *Civilisation and its Discontents* (standard edition, 21, pp.1–273). London: Hogarth.

Gottman, J.M. & Silver, N. (1999). *The Seven Principles for Making Marriage Work*. New York: Three Rivers Press.

Greenberg, L. & Johnson, S.M. (1988). *Emotionally Focussed Therapy for Couples*. New York: The Guilford Press.

Gurman, A. S. (ed.) (2008). *Clinical Handbook of Couple Therapy*. New York, London: The Guilford Press.

Gurman, A.S. & Fraenkel, P. (2002). The History of Couple Therapy: A Millennial Review. *Family Process*, 41(2), 199–259.

Johnson, S.M. (2008). *Hold Me Tight: Your Guide to the Most Successful Approach to Building Loving Relationships*. London: Little, Brown & Co.

Johnson, S.M. (2019) *The Practice of Emotionally Focused Couple Therapy: Creating Connection* (3rd ed.). London: Routledge.

Jones, E. & Asen, E. (2000). *Systemic Couple Therapy and Depression*. London: Karnac.

Lago, C. & Smith, B. (eds.) (2010). *Anti-Discriminatory Practice in Counselling and Psychotherapy*. London: Sage.

Lewin, K. (1952). *Field Theory in Social Work*. London: Tavistock.

Ludgate, J. & Grubr, T. (2018). *The CBT Couples Toolbox*. Eau Claire, WI: PESI Publishing.

McCann, D. (ed.) (2022). *Same-Sex Couples and Other Identities: Psychoanalytic Perspectives*. London: Routledge.

7

WHAT IS PSYCHODYNAMIC-PSYCHOANALYTIC COUPLE THERAPY?

INTRODUCTION

This chapter describes how psychoanalytic theories and psychodynamic approaches have influenced couple therapy. Psychodynamic-psychoanalytic therapies are also known as '**object relations therapies**' (ORT). The role of the '**object**' as a dynamic internal relationship, together with a definition of ORT, is covered in more detail below. For ease of reading, this chapter uses abbreviations. As well as ORT, ORCT is used for object relations couple therapy. Because the theories and therapy remain so closely linked, the chapter outlines the basic psychoanalytic beliefs before setting out a brief history of their use in ORCT and an explanation of the key ideas and terminology. A fictionalised account of the beginning of ORCT with a couple, Mandisa and Callum, illustrates these main features.

THEORETICAL CONTEXT

As readers navigate their way through the ideas explored in this chapter it may be helpful to have in mind the following:

- Because psychoanalysis has been developed and practised in so many ways over the past 120 years, it is hard to summarise usefully all its influences on couple therapy in one chapter. Additional applications, as found in attachment theory, mentalization, link theory, and selfobject theory are described in Chapter 8.

DOI: 10.4324/9781003313403-7

- The importance of the existence of an unconscious, which exerts an influence on our conscious lives, is fundamental to psychoanalysis and taken as read by therapists trained in this approach. This means that unconscious processes are seen to occur in *all* relationships, including therapeutic relationships, i.e., in couple therapy itself as well as in couple relationships.

- Psychoanalysis is a relational philosophy – describing human relations and the emotions through which they are expressed. This perception is also the starting point for psychoanalytic couple therapists whose work continually requires them to be alive to many forms of relationships: between people, the past and the present, inner and outer worlds, fantasy/phantasy (see the distinction later in the chapter) and reality, and between different ways of perceiving and describing human emotions, sexuality, and behaviour. Couple therapists thus creatively draw on a number of therapeutic approaches, and 'for better for worse', sometimes find themselves open to charges of eclecticism (see also Chapter 6).

- For ease of reading, psychoanalytic and psychodynamic couple therapy are here combined and abbreviated to ORCT.

- See also Sayers, (2021) for a more comprehensive introduction to Freudian psychoanalytic ideas.

OVERVIEW OF PSYCHOANALYTIC IDEAS AND PSYCHODYNAMIC PRACTICE

REPRESSION

Exploring the human mind, in both its conscious and unconscious lives, psychoanalysis supposes that in all of us life is experienced as if we inhabit two intermingling worlds – one internal and unconscious, the other external and conscious. '**Repression**' has an important role in bridging these two worlds. From the very start of our lives, because life can never be perfect, painful and adverse experiences are managed by sinking (or 'splitting off' and 'repressing') them into our unconscious mind, so putting them out of immediate reach. The internal world, however, still affects our perceptions of the external world, although in our conscious lives, we may not be aware, or be only partially aware, of it doing so.

OBJECTS

The internal world is populated by caricatured representations of relationships known as 'objects' which are formed early in our lives. They reflect our feelings about our relationships with significant others, such as mother, father, siblings, and parental couples, and they become templates for understanding other relationships which we later make or seek to make. The therapy that uses this way of understanding relationships has, from the 1930s, come to be called 'object relations therapy' (ORT). It is a departure within psychoanalytic thinking from Sigmund Freud's (1856–1939) earlier concentration on instinctual drives, focussing instead on what shapes the making of human relationships. Because of their prominence in ORT thinking, Ronald Fairbairn (1889–1964) and Melanie Klein (1882–1960) have become known respectively as the father and mother of this school of thought. Henry Dicks 'married' ideas from them both to formulate object relations marital therapy (1967).

Examples of internal objects:

- *The internal couple object* (or 'the couple in the mind') may be idealised as idyllically happy, or mistrusted as forever warring in a sadomasochistic struggle.
- *Maternal/paternal objects*: if we grew up having a continually difficult relationship with a controlling mother/father, in adult life, we might treat women/men in authority as if they are a controlling mother/father. The absence of a mother or father early in life might be also later be powerfully significant (See '**transference**' below.)

PROJECTION

Although split-off and repressed feelings are sunk into the unconscious, they can still cause discomfort. These feelings and the qualities that go with them may be unacceptable, because they are bad – perhaps angry or rejecting – or because they are good and we do not feel worthy of having them and thus of being loved. The term '**projection**' describes how we may deal with the discomfort by projecting them out – throwing them onto other people whom we then see as angry or rejecting, or even as saintly. People who closely observe close relationships notice how often this happens between partners, parents and children, and between siblings. It also occurs when more explicit communication is avoided.

PROJECTIVE IDENTIFICATION

Projecting feelings or attributes onto other people such as a partner becomes a powerful dynamic when that partner, for their own needs, repeatedly reacts in a way that plays out the role that is projected or offered. This is known as '**projective identification**'.

For example, in the case of couple A and B, A was neglected and felt unloved as a child. Forgetting her own needs and fearing that B will feel unloved, A slavishly devotes herself to B's needs as the 'needy one'. B, also neglected in childhood, enjoys being somewhat infantilised. When A gives birth to C, B becomes depressed and even more dependent on A. A has no life of her own.

PSYCHOTHERAPY

Applying ideas about the unconscious to therapy, Freud and Carl Jung (1875–1961) believed that we can access the internal world in our dreams and through an intensive experience of free-floating talking therapy with an analyst who is trained to understand the meaning of what is said. The talking creates a multi-dimensional picture drawn between internal and external worlds, past and present, reality and fantasy/phantasy. (Here there is a distinction between 'fantasy' as a conscious imagining, and 'phantasy' as an unconscious imagining). Therapy's task is to help the individual or the couple to find a balance between their experience of external reality and the disturbing feelings arising from their troubled, unconscious worlds. Realisations that come from talking may enable a person to make sense of, and thus come to terms with, conflicts in their everyday experience.

PSYCHODYNAMIC THERAPY

Psychodynamic therapy is a talking therapy that also draws on psychoanalytic thinking about the human mind. It puts less emphasis than psychoanalysis on unconscious influences, to focus more on conscious perceptions of the impact of the past on the present and of the external world on our emotional lives.

Psychoanalytic and/or Psychodynamic Therapy – Similarities and Differences

Some people regard these two approaches to therapy as inter-changeable, but there are differences as well as similarities. In comparing them, it may be helpful to envisage a bridge between them, on which sit the several ways of practising therapy that can trace their roots back to ideas shaped by Freud, Jung, and their followers. Practitioners on this bridge share many fundamental ideas, but may describe themselves, variously, as psychoanalysts, analytical psychologists, psychoanalytic psychotherapists, or psy-chodynamic therapists depending on their training, the frequency of sessions they recommend, and the degree to which they focus on the influence of the unconscious, or involve awareness of the external world in the therapy. Importantly, all object rela-tions-based training programmes, including for ORCT, require trainees to experience individual personal psychotherapy.

Couple therapists have found themselves in an interesting position in the family of psychoanalytic psychotherapies, moving back and forth on the bridge. Adapting to couples' needs requires flexibility regarding frequency of sessions offered; sessions are usually once, sometimes twice per week. Like psychodynamic psychotherapy, ORCT takes account of the significance of *both* the external world and of unconscious influences in couples' lives. ORCT has also benefited from numerous adaptations of post-Freudian thinking, showing that psychoanalytic concepts are not at all as fixed and antiquated as some would like to believe. (See Pickering, 2008 and also Chapter 8).

A BRIEF HISTORY OF ORCT: KEY INFLUENCES AND INFLUENCERS

Born Out of Individual Therapy

ORCT emerged in the 1930s and 1940s, based on psychoanalytic theories and practice originally designed for individuals (see also Chapters 4 and 6). Freud did not include adult couple relationships much in his thinking, although, interestingly, he did see the nursing couple of mother and baby as powerful in shaping an individual's development. And while Jung (1928) was a pioneer in perceiving the importance of the couple relationship, couple therapy at this time was still treated as a fringe activity in relation to fellow psychotherapies.

FINDING THE SHARED INTERNAL COUPLE

Addressing the epidemic in family breakdown in the 1930s and 1940s, pioneer therapists took ideas that psychoanalysts Fairbairn and Klein had developed from Freud, and applied them to couple relationships. Lily Pincus, in describing the '**couple fit**' (1960), Enid Balint, 'unconscious communication' (1968), and Dicks, 'the joint marital personality' (1967), laid the foundation stones in the UK for ORCT. A fundamental concept is that couples are seen as forming between them both conscious and unconscious links through which they communicate. Each partner has an 'internal world' which looks to make a 'fit' with that of their significant other. From this fit they co-create a shared internal couple with which to work out the still-to-be-resolved issues that both partners bring to their relationship. Thus, as Dicks pointed out, when a couple seeks therapy, the client (or patient) of the therapy is their *relationship*, not the individual partners of the couple.

USING AN OBJECT

A further important contribution came from Donald Winnicott (1896–1971) who described how the baby learns to "use … an object" (1971), an idea that has been applied to the close relationships such as those made in therapy or by couples. In the process of seeking out the mother, as 'object', the baby (or subject) comes to see her as separate and angrily attacks her. But when she (or the therapist, or partner) survives this and is not destroyed, the subject (baby or partner) learns that it is safe to be real in their angry feelings or aggression towards the separate other. The survival of the object shows that they are separate, outside the subject's control, and thus available for a *real* relationship.

For example, to revisit couple A and B (described on p. 90), A complains to T, their couple therapist, that since the birth of C, B, who is now depressed, does nothing to support them. B protests that A now neglects him for C. Hearing about their life and relationship before C's arrival, T helps them hear and to survive one another's angry disappointments. They begin to realise that as a childless couple they had enacted the idealised parent–child relationship each had longed for. Now they both have an opportunity to collaborate as parents to love and support C.

Not Just Freudian 'Old Hat' ...

Since its inception, ORCT has come a long way, endeavouring to absorb and adapt psychoanalytic thinking from across the world, in order to be alive to the ever-changing external environment. Hewison (2014) presents a current view of the couple as a 'meaning-making relationship'. ORCT's role has thus evolved; rather than addressing concerns about social breakdown, it now primarily fosters couples' potential to understand and reconcile their shared dreams with individual partners' personal goals.

... But Two Lively Age-Old Myths

Myths, dating from Ancient Greece, continue to serve as useful illustrations of contemporary human failings and dilemmas.

Oedipus

The ancient myth of Oedipus has had a starring role in psychoanalytic theories about sexual development. Some couple therapists find it useful for envisaging the growing child's experience of being excluded from their parents' sexual relationship (Grier, 2005). The model of a twosome from which a third is excluded, or (as in an eternal triangle) where there is a compulsion to include a third, is played out repeatedly in close relationships (see also Chapter 12). Couple therapy offers opportunities to experience three-person dynamics in active and creative ways, as well as inviting the couple to reconsider themselves as a threesome – a couple plus their relationship.

Narcissus and Echo

Narcissus, fell so much in love with his own reflection, he was oblivious of Echo's love for him. Pathological forms of '**narcissism**' (extreme self-obsession, rigidly controlling behaviour, resistance to change, lack of empathy), and of Echoism (obsessive focus on the needs of others at the expense of oneself) feature in codependent couple relationships (see Chapter 2) and greatly challenge couple therapists (Lackhar, 2004).

ORCT: THE MAIN FEATURES

Becoming a competent therapist usually requires ORCT training of at least two years for people who have already completed a prior compatible therapy training (see Chapter 13). The following summary lists features commonly met in ORCT. While there may appear to be several, they are often related in patterns:

- Transference and '**countertransference**'.
- '**Defences**' e.g., against loss, '**idealisation**', and the return of the repressed, prompting the question 'Why now?'
- Internal couple object and the couple fit.
- Projection and projective identification.
- '**Containment**' and the therapy as a '**container**'.
- A '**couple state of mind**'.
- Curiosity.

EXAMPLE OF EARLY ORCT MEETINGS WITH A FICTIONALISED COUPLE

MANDISA AND CALLUM: IN SUMMARY

Mandisa (early 30s) and Callum (late 40s), a heterosexual mixed-race couple, met in South Africa when Mandisa was a student teacher and Callum a college lecturer. Both were the eldest child in families where parents separated when they were in their teens. Together as a couple for eight years, they came to the UK three years ago to 'start a new life' and be closer to Callum's fourteen-year-old daughter by a previous marriage. Between them, they have a son (four years) and Mandisa's son (eleven years). Mandisa, finding it hard to settle, wants to return home. Both experienced depression following the breakdown of previous relationships. They meet with a couple therapist who is white, female, and in late middle age.

MANDISA AND CALLUM: IN DETAIL, WITH COMMENTARY ON THE THERAPIST'S OWN THOUGHTS

Before meeting, the couple wrote briefly to the therapist, introducing themselves and reasons for seeking therapy as set out above.

COMMENTARY: At the first meeting, there is a lot to take in, even on the doorstep. The therapist is immediately struck that Mandisa and Callum are a mixed-race couple, and wonders to herself why she is taken aback by this.

CALLUM: Takes charge, introducing them as 'Cal and Mandy'.

COMMENTARY: The therapist notes that his tone is bright, as if seeking immediate acceptance, and perhaps somewhat brittle. It is now evident that Mandisa, a black woman in her early thirties, is younger than Callum, a white man in his late forties, and from his accent a Scot. The overall impression is of an articulate, attractive couple who seem anxiously driven to start therapy.

MANDISA: Perched on her chair's edge, explains that the therapist has been highly recommended, which is very important to them, because they are both praying she will be able to help them. Mandisa looks anxiously at Callum for reassurance. He agrees.

COMMENTARY: Hearing about the recommendations and their anxious expressions of hope, the therapist initially feels flattered. This is quickly replaced by sinking feelings, realising that she has been idealised and is thus set up to fail. She notes Mandisa's apparent anxiety about Callum's reactions.

The therapist acknowledges their letter and its content, and asks if they want to say more.

CALLUM: He is upset to hear that Mandy wants to go 'home' to Cape Town. He knew that moving would be a challenge, but they had pinned their hopes on it. Now they both have work and a home in the UK for their family, it was a shock to discover that Mandisa seemed so set on going back – after *all* they had been through.

MANDISA: It breaks her heart to upset Cal but, after Christmas, she was suddenly aware how homesick she was. She hadn't realised it before, and now she finds herself crying every day. She has to think of her sons too ...

CALLUM: Breaks in, saying: But I'm their father too!

MANDISA: Now crying: I know, I know ...

CALLUM: I've tried so hard for you. We have a home here ...

MANDISA: *You* are at home here. *I* am not. That's the difference!

CALLUM: Looks nonplussed.

COMMENTARY: The therapist registers that within five minutes, what was an empty room is now filled with a maelstrom of hope and despair: a conflict of cultures, family upheaval in a bid for survival, loss, the needs of children versus the needs of adults, overwhelming demands. And in all of this, it might be so easy to neglect issues of race and power between two older white people and a younger black woman. There are oedipal issues too, with the threat of either the father or the younger woman being the silenced onlooker. The therapist needs to collect her thoughts so as not to lose what is important in the swirl of what is being spoken and felt. Much has been said, but much remains as yet unsaid. Beneath the veneer of their attractive presentation, there lies deep disquiet and uncertainty, leading them to invest heavily in a 'highly recommended' therapist.

One of the questions that the therapist will have to run past herself is, 'Who am I for this couple?' along with its mirror image, 'And who are they for me?' Both questions relate to 'transference'.

Now we step away from Mandisa and Callum to consider the significance of transference, countertransference, defences, idealisation, and containment.

TRANSFERENCE

Loosely defined as an impression, transference can be thought of as both a perception and a communication. It is generally only unconsciously registered. But, as in psychoanalysis, ORCT practitioners are taught to notice when it occurs. It is a state of mind that colours how we perceive other people, and is psychoanalytically understood to stem from earlier experiences of significant relationships which we carry with us throughout life.

The couple's transference to the therapist might be based on their previous relationships with older women whom they saw as wise, supportive, and perhaps maternal.

The therapist's transference to Mandisa and Callum might be based on couples she has known or met professionally before, and to whom she has warmed because they were engaging. As she recognises also from her own therapy, they might also remind her of mixed-race couples in her own family.

In both cases, the transference is a perception, which is often communicated non-verbally by the behaviour of both the couple and the therapist.

So What Does the Therapist Do?

When something is said by the couple that makes it clear what transference perspective both or one of them is using, it is helpful for the therapist to find a time be openly curious with them about it. (See below on '**interpretation**').

COUNTERTRANSFERENCE

Here, countertransference refers to the feelings that the therapist registers in response to the couple's experience of the hope they are investing in her. The therapist's countertransference (here in the form of a 'double-take' realisation and a sinking feeling) jars; it is as if a feeling of expectation, which she does not recognise as her own, has been laid upon her. When a therapist realises that this has occurred, it can be recognised as a significant communication from the couple of something that has not yet been put into words.

The therapist also has some sense of surprise – if not shock – that she should be taken aback that the couple was mixed-race, as if this was something she should have already known without being told. Did that come from herself, from unconscious racism? Or is it a countertransference clue to the couple's uncertainty about how they would be received? There were, after all, a number of ethnically different couples in the therapist's own family.

At this point, the therapist is caught up in noting her counter-transference to Mandisa and Callum as individuals. It takes longer for her to locate a sense of what they are telling her about themselves as a couple: that they are both anxious, both defensive. Why does Mandisa appear unsure of Callum's reaction to confessing their "prayers" for a solution? Why does Callum seem nonplussed, as if thrown, by Mandisa's change of mind? Is this a relationship in which one of them has to be in charge, as if *that* person's answers to problems are the only possible answers?

So What Does the Therapist Do?

There are a lot of reactions and thoughts to process; none are necessarily issues to raise immediately, but registering them may help to inform the therapist as the work progresses in thinking about the couple's concerns. Considering their defences may provide a way through.

DEFENCES

The therapist registers how much is at stake for Mandisa and Callum in seeking her help; so much that, straightaway, there is an attempt to protect their vulnerability against disappointment. Their idealisation of her, and Mandisa's prayerful need that the therapist will hear this, can be thought of as a defence against fears that there will be no happy solution.

In ORCT, as in psychoanalysis, the recognition of defences (in both the couple and the therapist) is fundamental to the work. Defences against vulnerabilities are essential for survival in all forms of life, and therapists respect the role defences play, regarding them as necessary while they can still operate creatively to sustain the individual or the couple. They become negative and outmoded, or 'beyond their use by date', when they prevent emotional growth, causing painful stuckness.

So What Does the Therapist Do?

The therapist's task is not to strip away defences, especially when they are serving a necessary role. If, however, they are preventing growth (for example, to avoid grieving about a shared loss), it is important that the therapist can talk about how painful the loss is and that although it is difficult, the couple will need time to grieve.

IDEALISATION

The therapist recognises the couple's wish to idealise her as a double-edged sword. Thinking positively, she understands Mandisa's anxious prayer of hope (perhaps on behalf of them both) that they can be helped. Negatively, however, their idealisation sets her up to meet an impossible standard; no-one is perfect and she is therefore sure to disappoint them.

Because of the hopes (and unspoken fear) that the client/couple has of therapy, therapists are frequently idealised. It is also an aspect of an inherent power dynamic in the relationship, in which a client (here a couple) is dependent on a therapist for their time, attention, and good will. Generally speaking, idealisation can be understood as a defence against hatred, if not fear. We put people on pedestals to place them out of our reach – both as idols who cannot be questioned and as demigods whom we cannot pull down. Therapy may be sought after, but we may hate being dependent on it in case it threatens our self-sufficiency. It can also be understood as a defence against hope; our supposed goals are made into impossible dreams, so we avoid being heartbroken when they fail because they were unattainable anyway.

So What Does the Therapist Do?

It is important that the therapist recognises when this is happening and be ready to 'look the gift horse in the mouth'. The unnamed future disappointment will need to be spoken about early on in a thoughtful and straightforward way. (See 'Interpretation').

CONTAINMENT

The therapist decides that she will need to make space before the session ends to say something to the couple about their idealisation of her, as well as to ask about the significance of racial differences for them. But she understands that first they will need space to tell their story and allow them to know that their distress has been empathically heard before she can raise important issues in what risks being an insensitive way. In other words, she needs to be 'containing'.

Containment is a state of mind that all therapists in psychoanalytic therapeutic relationships try to create in order to work effectively. It was most powerfully described by the psychoanalyst Wilfred Bion (1897–1979) who identified its essential role in infants' emotional development. When a mother (or carer) can hear and accept the baby's distress, and can let the baby know this by soothing, they can contain the raw pain of the distress and feed back a sense that it is, after all, manageable. (It is as if the pain has been 'metabolised' and returned in a 'de-toxified' form). If a mother (or carer) is unable to hear and metabolise the pain, the baby is left with an uncontained (i.e., undigested and indigestible) experience, and feels rage, bewilderment, and rejection. If this becomes the pattern of the baby's early experience of relationships, it subtly, but powerfully, affects all later relationships. Whenever the child seeks the containment they need, they may also defend against the anticipated rejection by setting up a disappointment; either demanding too much or by being self-sufficient.

So What Does the Therapist Do?

Containment becomes the basis of therapeutic relationships. When a therapist shows that they hear, accept, and want to understand another's experience, a sense of trust may very gradually be established, and so repair a broken belief about relationships; they can, after all, be creative rather than destructive. This process usually requires a series of patient responses and observations from the therapist; sometimes it involves quiet attentive listening; sometimes considered, thoughtful interpretations (see 'Interpretation' below).

Returning to Mandisa and Callum

The therapist invites Mandisa and Callum to say more about their concern.

CALLUM: He feels at a loss to understand why Mandy has decided against all that they had planned together. He looks flat, defeated.

MANDISA: But we didn't really plan it together. It was really your idea to come to Scotland. I went along with it because I thought finding your family again would make you happy. *She turns to the therapist to explain:* Cal was quite depressed in South Africa. He had to take sick leave, like before when he was at university. And his parents said 'Come home'. But now I know I can't be happy here, it's not my home. I only realised after Christmas how much I missed Cape Town and my family there. OK – they're not perfect, far from it, but I have to do so much to fit in here, I feel I am losing who I am. You even changed my name for your mother's sake ...

COMMENTARY: The therapist quietly registers the heavy sense of loss; loss pervades everything: home, family, identity.

CALLUM: We agreed to keep my mother out of it...

MANDISA: I know, but I feel she doesn't accept that *we* are a family now; she doesn't want me ... or the boys really. I don't want them to have to grow up all the time having to try to work out how best to fit in.

CALLUM: *Looks deflated.*

MANDISA: It's not your fault.

CALLUM: I know ... we started out with high hopes ... I still don't get where I – we – where it went wrong ...

COMMENTARY: The therapist decides that it is time to let the couple know something of what she has understood from their interaction and that means acknowledging a number of the issues the couple have raised. There may be too many to speak about all at once, but ideally, she should combine some in a way that will chime with the couple's feeling about their difficulties.

INTERPRETATION

Interpretation is seen to be a key aspect of psychoanalytic practice, especially where it brings into the open issues that were previously unconscious or only partially recognised. In couple therapy, interpretation is especially useful in helping the couple to be aware of how their relationship operates both consciously and unconsciously to help them, together and separately, to make sense of their lives.

So What Does the Therapist Do?

Interpretations should always be offered, rather than declared. They demonstrate how the therapist is thinking, and model a way of being curious in a non-intrusive way. They seek to engage the couple in a conversation, offering an impression of how their relationship appears to an outsider, and what *it* might say for itself, if given a voice.

The therapist tries this interpretation:

THERAPIST: I have been thinking as you have been speaking. I am struck that you have both spoken about having 'high hopes' – for therapy and for moving to UK. It seems as if you have come to a difficult crossroads and it's not at all straightforward which way to go – there's a lot hanging in the balance for you both and your children. Couple therapy can't do everything, but you are right to have come, because it might help the three of us to think together to support your relationship. I wonder if *it* is feeling quite burdened just now?

You stressed the importance of finding someone well recommended. I wonder if you were afraid that a white therapist wouldn't understand the pressures you face as a mixed-race couple? That's a realistic fear, because we are all limited by our experience. I shall do my best, but I'm aware that my limitations may disappoint you. You have already had to make some big choices in your lives, and often couples in your position find themselves depending a lot on a wider family. From what you have said, however, I wonder whether between you, you actually feel on your own – there's a lot at stake for your family, but how much support is there for you as a couple? Do you get the space you need to work things out between you?

The therapist notes that Mandisa and Callum both look more relaxed and ready to explain more.

CALLUM: It's hard with the children to find time on our own, and everyone in my family is ready to tell us what to do. Mandisa, your family gave you a hard time when we got together. But I know you are missing them and wanting to make it up with them.
MANDISA: Nods, and smiles tearfully.
THERAPIST: Would you both like to tell me more about how you met and got together?

CURIOSITY

Getting to know more about what has brought the couple to therapy and what style of relating the therapist practises is very much the order of the day.

Curiosity is increasingly appreciated as a relational stance that is at the heart of a psychoanalytic approach. It is sometimes expressed as a quiet, expectant waiting to hear, wanting to know. When more than two people are in the room, the therapist usually takes the lead in inviting people to speak, and prompting quiet partners to draw them in. The aim is to model a desire to relate, to ask about what the couple may be afraid to talk about, but without interrogating them as if they are on trial.

So What Does the Therapist Do?

Learning more about the couple's history and each partner's upbringing and family takes time. Some therapists like to do it systematically, others build a picture like a mosaic. The past, in this sense, is not 'another country', but seen as part of the picture of the present. Assembling that picture should feel as if it is part of telling the couple's story, not like a medical history-taking. Some therapists like to engage couples in drawing a genogram (see Chapter 9); others prefer to confine that to their own note-taking.

COMMENTARY: Having gathered more background and the impression that the couple want to continue to meet, the therapist contracts with Mandisa and Callum to meet again the following week, with a view to deciding then what further arrangements to make.

AFTER THE SESSION

The therapist makes notes to collect her thoughts on issues she plans to discuss in supervision. Although an experienced therapist, she values the discipline of meeting regularly with a colleague who can both challenge and support her. It is especially useful when considering work with a newly referred couple. Writing the notes, as listed below, helps the therapist to formulate her experience, making sense of the session with some new insights about it. This is often referred to as a 'process recording'.

THE THERAPIST'S NOTES – AMPLIFIED FOR READERS' INFORMATION

1. *Immediate sense (my countertransference to C & M)*: a heavy sense of loss. The high hopes of creating a bright future, against all the odds, risk being dashed. Losses of identity, pride, and family are real.

   Desperate hope: I so want it to work out for them, to do all I can. Ah! Is this a desire to *rescue* them? Whose wish is this? Is my/their wish to rescue part of their couple fit?

   Why so surprised by their racial difference! This needs more thinking about …

   The idealisation 'elephant trap'… Might idealisation also be part of their couple fit?

2. *In what ways are they a couple?* M wants to return to S Africa, even at the expense of breaking up the family? Do they have, or could they develop, a **creative couple state of mind** (Morgan, 2005) so they could contain one another in their relationship, and could their relationship be strong enough to contain them? It has been tested by periods of depression in them both and will need time to recover to show that it can be repaired to support them.

3. *Why now?* What has provoked this crisis now? Might Dicks' idea about the 'return of the repressed' in couples be helpful? They came to UK to rescue 'high hopes' during an idealised 'honeymoon period'. Is their post-Christmas crisis now, an instance of the old 'seven year itch' idea, when relationships start to wear thin and break down? Is it now challenging them to re-assess shared idealised assumptions, made when they met, about what they could achieve together? Did they both repress their separate disappointments growing up, realising that they alone as eldest children could not recreate family togetherness and a stable home? Christmas has reminded M of the loss of her family, and of her identity. Has this broken

through the idealised façade around C's promise of 'home' and family?

4. *Immediate tasks for the therapy*: M & C will need space to mourn their shared and separate losses and to decide whether they want to forge a renewed family together. Couple therapy may prove the container to enable them to do so.

CONCLUSION

The complex and intricate tasks of ORCT rightly require much longer consideration than this brief chapter allows (although some other applications are summarised in Chapter 8.) Many of the concepts described are linked and can be seen as processes in a chain reaction. Most of them require a lot of thought on the part of the therapist. In the discussion of the case above, the question, 'So what does the therapist do?' is frequently asked. It is noted that when more than two people are engaged in a therapy, the therapist often finds themselves being more active, as if directing the players. There are times when it is important not merely to witness, but to 'do' – i.e., to act by offering an interpretation. Yet the practice of therapy is generally more about *being* than *doing*; being containing while being authentic is more therapeutic than falling into the trap of trying to rescue. Some of the difficulties of maintaining this stance are explored in Chapter 10.

LET US ASK OURSELVES ...

- What is the most difficult concept in ORCT to understand or recognise when meeting with a couple?
- How might having experienced personal therapy help us when meeting couples in therapy?

CHAPTER SUMMARY

- This chapter describes how psychoanalytic theories and psychodynamic approaches have influenced 'object relations couple therapy' (ORCT). Beginning by outlining some basic psychoanalytic concepts, such as projection, projective identification, and use of an object, it briefly introduces key contributors. The myths of Oedipus and Narcissus also illustrate ideas and terminology used in ORCT.

- A fictionalised account of the first meeting of a couple and their therapist illustrates the main features, including transference, countertransference, defences, idealisation, containment, interpretation, and curiosity. Each is described and defined, asking what response the therapist might make.
- The therapist's processing of the experience after the session is discussed.

HAVE YOU READ?

Two books explore whether stability and security are compatible bed-fellows with romance and passion:

Mitchell, S.A. (2003). *Can Love Last? The Fate of Romance Over Time*. New York: Norton.
Perel, E. (2006). *Mating in Captivity: Reconciling the Erotic and the Domestic*. New York: Harper Collins.

REFERENCES

Balint, E. (1968). Unconscious Communication Between Husband and Wife. In: S. Ruszczynski (ed.) (1993). *Psychotherapy with Couples* (pp. 30–43). London: Karnac.
Dicks, H. (1967). *Marital Tensions*. London: Tavistock.
Grier, F. (2005). *Oedipus and the Couple*. London: Karnac.
Hewison, D. (2014). Projection, Introjection, Intrusive Identification, Adhesive Identification. In: D.E. & J.S. Scharff (eds.) *Psychoanalytic Couple Therapy: Foundations of Theory and Practice* (pp. 158–169). London: Karnac.
Jung, C.G. (1928). Marriage as a Psychological Relationship. In: *Contributions to Analytical Psychology* (pp. 189–203). London: Kegan Paul, Trench, Trubner & Co.
Lackhar, J. (2004). *The Narcissistic Borderline Couple*. New York: Brunner Routledge.
Morgan, M. (2005). On Being Able To Be a Couple: The Importance of a 'Creative Couple' in Psychic Life. In: F. Grier (ed.) *Oedipus and the Couple* (pp. 9–30). London: Karnac.

Pickering, J. (2008). *Being in Love: Therapeutic Pathways through Psychological Obstacles to Love.* London: Routledge.

Pincus, L. (ed.) (1960). *Marriage: Studies in Emotional Conflict and Growth.* London: Institute of Marital Studies.

Sayers, J. (2021). *Sigmund Freud: The Basics.* London: Routledge.

Scharff, D.E. & Scharff, J.S. (2014). *Psychoanalytic Couple Therapy: Foundations of Theory and Practice.* London: Karnac.

Winnicott, D.W. (1971). The Use of an Object. In: *Playing and Reality* (pp. 86–94). London: Tavistock.

8

FURTHER COUPLE THERAPIES LINKED TO PSYCHOANALYSIS

INTRODUCTION

Following the description given in Chapter 7 of the influence of psychoanalytic theories on '**Object relations**' couple therapies (ORCT), this chapter outlines four further adaptations of psycho-dynamic-psychoanalytic therapy:

1. Attachment theory and theorists.
2. Mentalization-based therapy, developed in the UK to support work with highly conflicted couples.
3. Link theory, followed especially in Europe and South America.
4. Selfobject couple therapy, practised principally in North America.

As in Chapter 6, where different modalities of couple therapy are summarised, here these additional applications of psychodynam-ic-psychoanalytic approaches in ORCT are each briefly defined and categorised under three headings:

1. Brief background history.
2. Principal ideas used in couple therapy.
3. Sources of further information.

PRELIMINARY THOUGHTS

Do Adaptations add Value?

Ideally, psychological theories are continually tested. Their original concepts may remain sound for some practitioners, such that some may even consider it heresy to change or challenge them.

DOI: 10.4324/9781003313403-8

For others, their continuing validity depends on whether they remain helpful in processing experiences of an ever-changing world, and can take account of continual discoveries of previously undescribed phenomena. If they need to be adapted, can this be done without dismantling their core hypotheses? In relation to adapting psychoanalytic ideas in the context of couple therapy, two examples stand out:

1. Embracing therapy for couple relationships, compared with considering the relationship an individual has with themselves or their therapist, has required new dimensions of thought and a new vocabulary.

2. Ideas about human relationships travelled with European immigrants to other parts of the world and, over time, psychological theories were adapted to fit the new communities established there. There has been some continuing cross-continental dialogue in psychoanalytic communities, but also some 'casting off' by some practitioners keen to establish their separate identities. As with other therapies, this development has also shaped couple therapy, as can be seen in Latin America with link theory, and in North America with selfobject therapy.

While considering each of the four adaptations of psychoanalytic thinking listed above, it may also be helpful to remember the possible 'functions' for a therapist in their adoption of a particular approach, i.e., what does following that way of thinking and practising *do* to support a therapist as they meet with a distressed, conflicted couple? (See also Chapters 4 and 5).

- It grounds the therapist with an anchor when the couple's thinking is chaotic.
- The therapist is not alone; they feel part of an authorised, respected community.
- The way of thinking chimes with and validates their experience.
- The particular school of thought offers a sense of identity and opportunity for belonging, all the more vital when faced with clients whose own sense of identity and feelings of belonging are insecure and challenging.

ATTACHMENT THEORY AND THEORISTS

Brief Background History

Attachment theory was developed by John Bowlby (1907–1990), a psychiatrist and psychoanalyst, and Mary Ainsworth (1913–1999), a developmental psychologist. Working closely together, both maintained that infants' experiences of receiving care had profound effects on the way they gave and received care in relationships in adult life. The concept of a '**secure base**', first described by Ainsworth, was later used as the title of Bowlby's famous collection of lectures setting out how attachment theories are used in therapy (Bowlby, 1988).

The 'secure base' – the source of security to which we turn in times of stress and danger – has become a commonly used metaphor when referring to basic psychological needs. From Ainsworth's studies observing how infants and children responded to a 'Strange Situation Test', Bowlby described patterns of behaviour which, from early years, would become 'internal working models' for understanding and managing dependency situations of security, separation, and loss. These attachment responses, respectively termed, 'secure', 'anxious', 'avoidant', and 'disorganised', are also observed in adult relationships, where rather than seeking security, the main driver of attachment is sexual attraction.

Although Bowlby's theories are essentially psychoanalytic (Fonagy, 1999), in his understanding of the crucial role of the internal world and the function of '**defences**', some members of the psychoanalytic community have marginalised him, because of his criticisms of Sigmund Freud's theories on infantile sexuality and Melanie Klein's on phantasy. Nevertheless, because of their foundation in action research and wide applicability in child, couple, and family therapies, attachment theories continue to be drawn on in both therapy and research. An example of the latter is the work of Philip Cowan and Carolyn Cowan, whose 'Becoming a Family' project has, since 1975, continued a longitudinal study of becoming parents on couples and families (Cowan & Cowan, 2000).

Attachment theory offers a universally applicable, coherent way of understanding of human relationships, which some therapists find more accessible than other psychoanalytic approaches. There is considerable compatibility between them, such that it sometimes seems that therapists trained in either attachment or object relations are describing the same phenomena, albeit in different terms or from a slightly different perspective. Indeed, some therapists openly draw on both ways of thinking.

Attachment theories have also contributed to other therapies, notably emotionally focussed couple therapy (Johnson, 1996) and mentalization (see below).

Principal Ideas Used in Couple Therapy

- The 'secure base' is a refuge first sought by infants or growing children in times of stress and danger; even if it offers little or no security, paradoxically, it will still be turned to if it is all that is available. For example, an abusive parent may still function as a child's secure base. Bowlby contended that attachment – the desire to be close to a caregiver – is increased when we are afraid or threatened. In adult life, vulnerability may cause us to stick to a partner, even when that partner presents a threat. In *A Secure Base* (1988), Bowlby defines the therapist's chief task as the creation of a secure base from which their clients can safely explore painful aspects of their lives.

  Thus, the concept of the secure base, as both a literal and metaphorical description of couple, family, parent-child, and therapeutic relationships, can be widely applied. In *this* book, it variously illustrates:
    - The desire to create a parental couple;
    - The contract between couple and therapist;
    - The '**therapeutic frame**';
    - The couple's relationship as a supportive third party;
    - A good enough beginning to couple therapy; and
    - The therapy itself as a continuing reflective space in which to reconsider conflict.
- The 'internal working model' neatly describes the dynamic interactions of the internal world, similar to the concept of object relating. The growing child uses the model to make sense of their dependent relationships, and defensively to predict whether dependency will prove either dependable and

sympathetic, or unreliable and/or abusive. To hold onto a relationship, the child also learns to suppress experiences if their caregiver cannot tolerate certain behaviours, such as, for example, protests about being abandoned. This leads the grown person in later life to have a more limited 'vocabulary' or range of expression of feelings with which to relate emotionally with their partner.

•   The four attachment responses or styles have been further described as: 'secure', 'anxious' or 'preoccupied', 'avoidant' or 'dismissive', and 'disorganised' or 'fearful–avoidant'. These classifications of behaviours are the outward expressions of the internal working model. These patterns of relating, particularly with a partner, can be identified and are thus useful in assessing a couple's difficulties. The classification also provides researchers with additional measures when studying relationships.

•   Bowlby's listening style reflects one which many in ORCT aspire to. He stresses that rather than '"I know, I'll tell you", the stance I advocate is one of "You know, you tell me".' (1988, p.151). This supports the client (couple) in discovering for themselves how their past models have contributed to their present ways of relating. This then enables them to own the process of freeing themselves so that they can restructure their relationship; the therapist's role is to support the client in a natural process of self-healing. Applied to couple therapy, the role becomes more one of guidance than direction.

Sources of Further Information

•   Bowlby (1988).
•   Clulow (2001a).
•   O'Shaughnessy et al. (2023).

With particular regard to emotionally and physically abusive relationships see:

•   The play: *Who's Afraid of Virginia Woolf?* (Albee, 1962)
•   The film: *Who's Afraid of Virginia Woolf?* (Nichols, 1966).
•   The commentary by Clulow (2001b).

MENTALIZATION

BRIEF BACKGROUND HISTORY

Mentalization – the ability to understand what is happening in one's own or another's mind – has been dubbed the capacity 'to think about thinking' or for 'understanding misunderstanding'. When feelings run high that capacity decreases. The significance of this was emphasised by the psychoanalyst, Peter Fonagy, when drawing attention to the lack of mentalization in people with borderline personality disorder (BPD) (Fonagy, 1989). People with BPD experience extreme changes in mood, react impulsively, and struggle to create stable, close relationships. With couples in mind, this means that a partner with BPD is likely to find it difficult both to live in a relationship *and* to live without one. Although these difficulties may present more in one partner than another, the fact that they are a couple means that their relationship can be considered to be 'on the borderline' (Nyberg & Hertzmann, 2019).

Fonagy also identified the links between mentalization and attachment theories when considering trauma in female victims of aggression (Fonagy, 1999). Since then the concept has been used to devise mentalization-based therapy (MBT) (Bateman & Fonagy, 2012) – talking therapy programmes designed to make therapy more accessible to people with BPD. This has also been applied by Tavistock Relationships to develop a specific therapy for couples (MBT-CT) and parents (MBT-PP) whose couple and family relationships are undermined by violence and who find conventional therapy too distressing (see also Appendix 2).

PRINCIPAL IDEAS USED IN COUPLE THERAPY

- Promoting 'reflective function' in the couple – the ability to tolerate thinking about what we and others are thinking and feeling. This ability is often disabled in partners who have BPD, when partners perpetually fight about their children, and when there is situational couple violence.
- Promoting 'reflective function' in the therapist through preparatory training, ongoing peer support, and supervision to enable the therapist to maintain a 'thinking mind'. This is vital when working closely with couples where this capacity is continually challenged or is lost.

- Understanding 'acting out': when a person cannot think about (mentalize) an extreme feeling, such as anger or fear, it may feel so catastrophic that they try to get rid of it by behaving it or by provoking others to behave it, e.g., through self-harm, violence to others, or drug-use. Understanding the motivation – i.e., the desire for relief from intolerable stress, rather than malevolence – is very important.
- Focussing on the couple's abilities to process what is happening between them. This may mean:
  - Not asking them to talk about experiences, whether from childhood or the recent past, which were traumatic or which still arouse strong feelings;
  - Not offering '**interpretations**' or commenting on '**transference**' and '**countertransference**' issues (see Chapter 7) until the therapist is confident that they can be received as supportive, rather than provocative.
- '**Problem formulation**': working out and agreeing with the couple the central issue to be worked on within a limited time frame of up to twenty sessions. If one partner is unable, through anxiety, to attend some sessions, separate meetings can be arranged on the understanding that the therapist will hold the absent partner in mind.
- Addressing challenging perceptions. Taking in another's thoughts creates tensions and is sometimes terrifying:
  - For the couple, perceiving one's partner as separate and different;
  - For the therapist, perceiving the couple relationship as combining two different partners.

SOURCES OF FURTHER INFORMATION

- Bateman & Fonagy (2012).
- Nyberg & Hertzmann (2019).

LINK THEORY

BRIEF BACKGROUND HISTORY

Link theory ('*el vínculo*') is a branch of psychoanalytic thinking devised in Argentina by Enrique Pichon-Rivière (1907–1977), who was inspired by object relations, anthropology, and field theory. His interest in applying psychoanalysis to a broad spectrum of relationships has given link theory currency in couple and family therapy, and made it influential in Europe as well as Latin America. Yet *el vinculo* has been described as 'one of the most powerful concepts that English-speaking psychoanalysts and therapists have never heard of' (Scharff, 2016, p.157).

PRINCIPAL IDEAS USED IN COUPLE THERAPY

- All personal relationships are defined by a link which is formed by the speech and interactions between people. People forge the links, and in turn are moulded psychologically by them, in a continual chain reaction. Making a relationship with another who is necessarily different from ourselves challenges our sense of self and thus continually redefines us. The link involves both the internal and the external worlds of the partners, and thereby those of their respective families too.
- The link runs in two directions: the 'vertical axis', which links previous, present, and future generations, and the 'horizontal axis', which links individuals, couples, and families, rippling out to groups and society beyond. We see in this how couples are part of a complex system of interrelationships, affected by and expressing transgenerational links as well as powerful social dynamics.
- Therapy is a 'spiralling' process with which the therapist identifies the difficulty via interpretations that 'interrupt' the 'existent' system to allow in a new 'emergent' one. The therapist's role can thus be considered as more challenging than reflective.
- The 'identified patient' is seen as a powerful embodiment of a family's problem and an important messenger in expressing unresolved issues in the couple and family system.

SOURCES OF FURTHER INFORMATION

Scharff & Scharff (2011)

SELFOBJECT COUPLE THERAPY

BRIEF BACKGROUND HISTORY

Heinz Kohut (1913–1981) devised self psychology as a new way of using psychoanalysis to explore relationships, placing a focus on the self as the central figure. The concept of the selfobject describes the part of oneself which from infancy is invested in others so that they are perceived as part of oneself. The selfobject thus becomes part of all close relationships; when the other fails to respond in the ways that we have identified with, unless there is also empathic understanding, the self feels threatened or injured by that failure.

PRINCIPAL IDEAS USED IN COUPLE THERAPY

- In addition to emphasising the corrective power of empathy in therapy, Kohut further described three kinds of transference (see also Chapter 7) which the therapist should seek to recognise and nurture:
  - 'Mirroring', i.e., tuning in to non-verbal behaviour;
  - 'Idealising', i.e., the partner is special;
  - 'Twinship or alter ego', i.e., 'we are as one' (Kohut, 1984). This aims to restore the couple's selfobject in supporting their relationship.
- Exploring why the selfobject no longer functions as it did when the couple fell in love, sometimes focussing on one partner's difficulties.
- *Selfdyad*: Richard Zeitner (2012) added this concept to self psychology, extending the idea of the selfobject to create a bridge between individual and couple therapy, and building on Henry Dicks' idea of the 'joint marital personality' (see also Chapter 7). The selfdyad is sustained in therapy by the therapist's empathic recognition of the three transferences set out above.

SOURCES OF FURTHER INFORMATION

- Zeitner (2012).

LET US ASK OURSELVES ...

- Why do you think some therapists are so opposed to adaptations of therapy?
- What cultural influences have you found most significant in the practice of therapy you are most familiar with?

CHAPTER SUMMARY

- This chapter briefly discusses the purposes served by adapting theories.
- It then outlines four additional methods of couple therapy that have been influenced by psychoanalytic thinking: attachment theory, mentalization-based therapy, link theory, and selfobject couple therapy.
- Each is briefly defined and categorised in terms of a brief background history, the principal ideas used applied to couple therapy, and sources of further information.

REFERENCES AND FILMOGRAPHY

Albee, E. (1962). *Who's Afraid of Virginia Woolf?* New York: Atheneum Books.

Bateman, A. & Fonagy, P. (2012). *Handbook of Mentalizing in Mental Health Practice.* New York: American Psychiatric Publishing.

Bowlby, J. (1988). *A Secure Base: Clinical Applications of Attachment Theory.* London: Routledge.

Clulow, C. (ed.) (2001a). *Adult Attachment and Couple Psychotherapy.* London: Brunner Routledge.

Clulow, C. (2001b). 'Attachment, Narcissism, and the Violent Couple'. In: *Adult Attachment and Couple Psychotherapy* (pp. 133–151). London: Brunner Routledge.

Cowan, C.P. & Cowan, C.A. (2000). *When Partners Become Parents: The Big Life Change for Couples.* Mahwah, NJ: Lawrence Erlbaum.

Fonagy, P. (1989). On Tolerating Mental States: Theory of Mind in Borderline Patients. *Bull. Anna Freud Centre,* 12, 91–115.

Fonagy, P. (1999). The Male Perpetrator: The Role of Trauma and Failures of Mentalization in Aggression Against Women: An Attachment Perspective. *The 6th John Bowlby Memorial Lecture.* London: The Centre for Attachment-based Psychoanalytic Psychotherapy.

Johnson, S.M. (1996). *Emotionally Focussed Marital Therapy.* New York: Brunner Mazel.

Kohut, H. (1984). *How Does Analysis Cure?* Chicago: University of Chicago Press.

Nichols, M. (dir.) (1966). *Who's Afraid of Virginia Woolf?* [film]. Warner Bros.

Nyberg, V. & Hertzmann, L. (2019). Mentalization-Based Couple Therapy. In: A. Balfour, C. Clulow, & K. Thompson (eds.) *Engaging Couples* (pp. 130–143). Abingdon: Routledge.

O'Shaughnessy, R., Berry, K., Dallos, R., & Bateson, K. (2023). *Attachment Theory: The Basics*. New York and London: Routledge.

Scharff, D.E. (2016). The Contribution of Enrique Pichon-Rivière. *Couple and Family Psychoanalysis*, 6(2), 153–158.

Scharff, D.E. & Scharff, J.S. (2011). *The Interpersonal Unconscious*. Lanham, MD: Jason Aronson.

Zeitner, R. (2012). *Self Within Marriage: The Foundation for Lasting Relationships*. New York: Routledge.

9

FIRST MEETINGS WITH A COUPLE

INTRODUCTION

Covering therapy's initial phase of up to three meetings, this chapter looks at what happens in a couple's first meetings with a therapist and the importance of these meetings in setting the tone for their work together. Addressing this 'consultation phase', the chapter begins by describing important features established at the outset, such as the **'therapeutic frame'**, contract making, assessment, and the place of **'interpretation'**. Illustrations are provided by vignettes. Other methods of assessment offer additional perspectives.

THE VERY FIRST MEETING

This has many of the hallmarks of a blind date and, as when couples first meet or are on a first date, a number of assumptions are made. If the relationship is to last long enough to meet their needs, it will be important to check out the usefulness of any assumptions early on. The first meeting might also be compared with a job interview, although both the therapist and the couple may feel that they are on trial and seeking acceptance. It takes courage on the part of the couple to seek an outsider's view of their situation.

Filled with anticipation and apprehension, first meetings are understandably anxious times for all parties. The couple may struggle with competing feelings of hope and despair, while the therapist is concerned to remember all that should be conveyed, as well as to be open to whatever is said. With all the reasons why couples find it difficult to commit to therapy, as set out in Chapter 3, it is salutary for the therapist to be aware that the couple may have had to talk themselves into coming, and that much hangs in the balance for them.

The couple's story is usually painful, sometimes too painful to tell in full at this stage. The therapist may be the only person who has heard their grief. Being ready to take in so much feeling (and mixed feelings), as well as being appropriately business-like, means the therapist will need a clear head. They must remember that as the host, their role is to provide a calm, welcoming approach and a safe place to talk. All the while, they must be ready to be real about whether they can truly offer the couple what they need.

In summary therefore, the main objective of this initial meeting, which may form part of a consultation phase (see below, and also Chapter 4), is to establish the footings for a trusting relationship which has the potential to continue for as long as is required. It is a time for enquiry from all parties about why they are meeting and whether this is going to be useful to them.

PREPARATION

Some significant steps can be taken in preparation for the therapy even before any meetings take place. For example:

- Couples may have researched what kind of therapy they are likely to get (see Chapter 4, 'Useful questions to ask').
- There may have been an initial explorative phone or email discussion to establish reasons for the referral.
- Some therapists may ask couples to write briefly in advance of meeting to explain reasons for seeking therapy and their hopes for any outcome.

All of this helps to foster the engagement between the couple and the therapist and will determine whether their relationship finds a good enough shared understanding to continue.

Some agencies use questionnaires – written or verbal – to learn more about their prospective clients. This pre-assessment can help to identify clients whose history of violence suggests that in joint sessions a partner may fear revealing the truth about their experience. In these circumstances, some agencies arrange to meet partners separately.

CONSULTATION PHASE

This phase of one to three meetings may prove sufficient to meet the couple's needs. Essentially, a consultation involves a process of assessment by both the couple and the therapist. It has these aims:

- To hear and clarify an understanding of the couple's difficulties and begin the process of making an assessment of the best way of working together.
- To establish a good 'fit' for the working relationship between the couple and the therapist.
- To make a contract that sets out a shared understanding of the arrangements for meeting.

THREE KEY FEATURES

1. *The therapeutic relationship as a 'frame'*: the concept of the 'therapeutic frame' is important in psychoanalytic thinking because it forms the basis of a therapeutic relationship (Scharff, 2014, pp.131–134). The frame describes a context for the therapy: when and where it will happen, the fee, and with what boundaries. Within the frame there is an explicit understanding that the therapy is for the *relationship*, not for the two individual partners attending together (see Chapter 3). Essentially, the partners have together brought their relationship for help. While the terms of the frame are firm, they need not be rigidly fixed, and can be open to some negotiation. In this way, holding the frame in mind models for the couple a way of relating to a relationship; it provides reliability while accepting the need for flexibility and the place of negotiation. The frame grounds the therapy on a '**secure base**' (see also Chapter 8), and allows couples the safety they need to explore previously unmanageable conflict.
2. *Contract making*: Contracts, written or verbal, literally spell out the 'frame' as a shared understanding of the terms of meeting

(see Chapter 4). The couple's ability to agree and keep to the terms of the contract may also usefully show how they feel about commitments in relationships.

3. *Assessment*: assessment is a process that happens continually throughout therapy, and not just a procedure to be completed at the beginning. While it might be most frequently thought of as something the therapist does, ideally both the couple and the therapist participate in considering, reconsidering, and sharing their understanding of the meaning of what has brought them to therapy and what might best be done to address it. Once the couple can own the assessment, they can participate as collaborators in the therapy.

ASSESSMENT: SOME SALIENT ISSUES

THE PLACE OF QUESTIONS

While some questions concerning basic information need to be asked openly, others, equally as important, can be held in the therapist's awareness – in their '**couple state of mind**' (Morgan, 2001), or in a 'bank' of issues to be curious about. A good therapist models a caring curiosity without becoming intrusive. Getting to know a couple involves being curious about many aspects of their lives. But pursuing such issues should never feel like an interrogation, and as if, rather than being open to the couple's story, the therapist is more interested in confirming their own impressions. Unless required by an agency, it is better not to depersonalise any history-taking by completing questionnaires during a meeting.

Three Essential Questions Guiding Recommendations for Therapy

- Do they (the couple) want it?
- Do they need it?
- Can they make use of it?

Answers to these three questions form the foundation of the therapist's initial assessment and are a useful test of whether couple therapy is the right course of action just now. The questions focus issues that should occupy the therapist:

- Are they ambivalent about committing themselves? If yes, why?
- Are they (or one partner) inhibited and/or put at risk because of the other's aggression? If yes, what security needs should be provided for?
- Are there significant issues of alcohol or drug use that mean that couple therapy may need to be postponed until that is no longer so?
- What is the main presented concern and might it mask others?
- Why have they come *now*?
- What is the feeling in the room, conveyed by the words used and the non-verbal communication?
- What is not being said? And what might I not be seeing?
- What are they hoping for? How do they see their future – together or separated?

Particular Questions for the Therapist

'In what ways are these two people a couple?' This is a central question for couple therapists (see also Chapter 2). Its intention is to help both therapist and couple to understand whether they will benefit from *couple* therapy, and in that sense is not personally discriminatory. It may be that individual therapy would prove the better option.

Some couple therapists may approach this by asking themselves, 'What are this couple's strengths?' This is in line with a systemic perspective when seeking to maximise positive rather than negative attributes.

Psychoanalytic therapists have pictured this as the couple having a 'couple state of mind' (see Chapter 7). Assessing early on in the therapy the two people's capacities for such a state of mind is thus important. It does not have to exist strongly at the start, but needs to be sufficiently present to be developed as a significant resource during and after therapy. The following two vignettes may help to illustrate the difference:

K and P arrived separately for their first appointment. K had come from an antenatal appointment and P had been visiting his sister. K anxiously sought **T's** (the therapist's) support, while P appeared distracted by his phone. They seemed ill at ease, making only brief eye contact with one another. K explained that they met six months ago when P moved into a flat she shared with two others. They had hit it off sexually. The pregnancy was unplanned, but K was keen to keep the baby. P wasn't sure as he planned to go travelling. K said she was in love with P, who replied that, yes, he liked K 'a lot', but did not want to settle down yet. T felt concerned for K and the baby, irritated with P's ambivalence, and powerless to help the two of them to 'make a match'.

S and J arrived separately for their first appointment, both coming from respective places of work. On arrival, each greeted the other and S asked J, 'Are you OK?' S looked anxiously at T (therapist) while J appeared somewhat flat. S said she and J had been together for four years and planned to get married. Then, a year ago, J's mother died by suicide and J became depressed and took sick leave from work. But S felt their difficulties were all her fault. Recently, they had been at a party and J left early. S had 'drunk too much' and flirted with a work colleague. A picture of them kissing was circulated by 'friends' on social media. S looked beside herself with shame; J looked collapsed and wounded. Both looked suddenly alone. T wondered what to say; there was so much pain. From the start, T sensed a desire to reconnect, but, underneath it, also unspoken grief and anger.

What would *you* recommend to K and P and to S and J?

K and P

It could be argued that, *overall,* K and P would find most benefit from individual therapy. While it is doubtful whether P would consider attending further therapy, without understanding more about his ambivalence, he should not be written off. With commitment issues approached cautiously, they might be willing to attend a further session together to discuss how they will both relate in future to K's pregnancy and their roles as parents.

S and J

There are several indications that S and J need time to talk together and would thus benefit from continued couple therapy on a time-unlimited basis. This would allow examination of their hope to marry in the context of the meanings for them both of S's behaviour at the party, of the loss of J's mother, and of their lack of a supportive social system around them.

THE USE OF INTERPRETATION

Interpretation (See also Chapter 7) is a technique valued as a crucial way of working by psychodynamic-psychoanalytic therapists. It aims to bring to the surface, and so make available for discussion and understanding, the underlying meanings of behaviour and experiences. The therapist's interpretations, where possible, use the couple's own words and metaphors to reflect back what the therapist has picked up from the couple through '**transference**' and '**countertransference**'. The therapist's focus on the couple's relationship should be explicit. Because interpretation is so much part of this way of working, it is important, early on, to assess how the couple responds to it. Does it help them to feel understood? Can they make use of it and therefore of this kind of therapy?

If not, the couple is unlikely to feel that a psychoanalytic kind of therapy is helpful, although they may do very well with one that uses a different approach.

The following are examples of the different interpretations that might be tried out with K and P and with S and J – the enquirers for couple therapy described above:

T's Possible Interpretation and Recommendations for K and P

T: It seems that, between you, it feels impossible to decide what to do. You didn't plan to have a baby together, and you feel differently about it and about whether now is the time for you to plan to be together, as a couple and as parents. It's a very big, life-changing decision to make, and one that you would both need to feel ready to go with. Whether you want to be a couple together is a decision that only you can make. The baby cannot make it for you, nor can I as a therapist. But you are both here, out of how you feel about one another. It might be important to take it in small separate steps. We could arrange to meet once or twice again to discuss whether you want to think together about the pregnancy in the first instance.

T's Possible Interpretation and Recommendations for S and J

T: I am struck by how painful all this is for you both to talk about. It feels as if something quite devastating has happened to you, and I am wondering how much you have been able to talk with one another about it? Thinking about it, you have both had the experience of being publicly shamed. I have the impression that both of you feel alone with your feelings, and almost as if your shared dream of being married has been trashed? You mention, but haven't spoken much about, what it meant to lose J's mother, and in that way, and about the effect on you both of J being depressed. Getting married was important to you, but something has changed that, and maybe S's flirtation at the party was a way of her asking what your relationship means to you both. And it is hard to ask such a question when you are grieving for someone dear to you and when you have been betrayed by your friends. I sense that you have both come because you care deeply about one another, but you need a space and enough time to explore things that have been too difficult to talk about.

It is relatively easy, of course, at a distance to compose a 'good enough' interpretation. But in the 'heat' of the meeting, the therapist has to keep as cool a head as possible to reflect back to the couple their impression of what they have heard. This is not always easy, and rather than being said all at once, the above suggested interpretations could be made as the session progresses. In any event, the couple may indicate that they cannot take in very much feedback. That will prove an important indication about the style of working they need, as well as predicting whether there is a good enough 'fit' between the couple and the therapist.

Using Other Frameworks to Assist Assessment

Classifications

A number of writers have classified couples' difficulties to help both couples and therapists decide what issues to focus on, or whether the relationship has any future. Notable examples are:

- Gottman and Silver (1999) identify 'Four Horsemen of the Apocalypse ... criticism, contempt, defensiveness, and stone-walling' as predictors of divorce. Based on many years' scientific research to classify the elements required for contented and lasting relationships, they detail the 'seven principles for making marriage work' with the aim of strengthening a couple's friendship, which they see as being at the heart of their relationship. These ideas are associated with the emotionally focussed therapy (EFT) school (see Chapter 6) and also contribute to the work of:
- Williams (2022). As well as communication, conflict resolution, culture, commitment, caring, couple's sexual relationship, contract, character, Williams adds an eighth – 'children'.

Different Dimensions

Other writers describe couple relationships as having different dimensions and use these in their understanding of couples' difficulties. A developmental perspective, which spans time from past to present, is adopted particularly by psychoanalytic, psychodynamic, and systemic thinkers. It views couple relationships themselves as having their own life cycle, growing from 'infancy' into maturity as they age. It is part and parcel of the key 'Why now?' question.

- Development is one of five dimensions listed by Crawley and Grant (2008), to be considered in assessment alongside cross-generational, communication, organisational, and ecological dimensions. The authors stress that it is important to consider the impact of gender norms and expectations and how these affect satisfaction in couples as their relationship develops. This multi-dimensional approach thus takes account of the environmental impact (i.e., the impact of the wider world) on the couple's relationship.

- Dorothy Freeman (1990), writing about short-term counselling, highlights four phases of marriage, each having difficulties that are peculiar to that point in the relationship life cycle.

  1. *The beginning phase*: a couple without children.
  2. *The child-rearing phase*: a couple with young children.
  3. *The middle phase*: a couple with teen-aged children.
  4. *The child-leaving phase*: couples whose children are about to leave, have left; and couples who are retired and on their own.

  As life expectancy increases, more couples are experiencing older age together. Couple therapists should expect to receive referrals from couples in their sixties and seventies who find themselves at odds in managing the particular challenges thrown up by new forms of dependency encountered in older age.

- Trans-generational links: noting the repetition across generations of relationship patterns is a past-present dimension useful to reveal in assessment. The discovery of such links is made through drawing a genogram, a technique initially described by McGoldrick and Gerson (1985).

ONLINE MEETINGS AND ASSESSMENT

For several years, therapeutic work has been increasingly conducted remotely using the telephone or screen. The necessity of online meetings, as a result of COVID-19 restrictions, increased and improved video links and, in turn, led to a consideration of how to adapt the familiar therapeutic frame. Meeting online has democratised therapeutic relationships, so that couples are freer to set their own boundaries. For example, instead of meeting in the therapist's consulting room, they might choose to speak from separate rooms in their house, from their bedroom to ensure privacy from the children, or from the park. Given all of this, the sound quality may be poor and the internet intermittent, and the scope of the screen does not allow a clear reading of body language.

Making an assessment in these circumstances can be challenging, and requires the therapist to be adaptable and to carry a strong sense of the therapeutic frame in the forefront of their mind. Therapists are challenged to have the confidence and authority to note and be curious about such issues as:

- Why does one partner fill most of the screen?
- Why does one partner lie back casually, while the other leans forward?
- Why does this couple allow their dog so often to intervene and interrupt them?
- Why do they come late and leave early?

Working online, the therapist has been invited into the couple's space and is presented with a picture of the couple that might otherwise not be so readily apparent. Visiting the couple at home may cause them to feel more vulnerable, more exposed, whereas meeting them on the therapist's territory may cause them to reveal how they react to a strange situation in strange surroundings. Each different venue offers the therapist different, but valuable, potential insights.

Other Takes / 'Snap Shots'

Doorstep Encounters

Whenever the therapist opens the door (or the screen) to receive the couple, be it at the first, or any subsequent meeting, they should always also be opening themselves to being aware of what the couple is bringing with them. As well as the words said, what feelings are communicated on the doorstep? How does the couple inhabit the space? These opening moments can be very telling; first impressions should be listened to as they often convey important feelings that risk being submerged by all that follows. Equally significant messages may be conveyed on the doorstep on leaving, when the therapist may receive the parting 'gift' of an impression left with them. There might be the slipped-in communication, 'By the way, we are not sure when we can come back as X has hospital appointments'. Or the couple who came in distress may leave relatively light-heartedly; or they may appear disappointed, their muttered 'Thanks' including an unspoken, 'But no thanks'.

Transference and Countertransference

Registering transference and countertransference can provide very useful clues to the therapist in assessing the relationship between the couple and between the couple and the therapist. Awareness of this way of communicating can help the therapist to understand the doorstep phenomena above.

As the session proceeds, and especially the first session when there seems to be so much to make sense of, it is important that the therapist can pause to take stock, to reflect on what has been said, and to tune in to transference and countertransference. Examples of this are given above in the vignette of K and P:

> T felt concerned for K and the baby, irritated with P's ambivalence, and powerless to help the two of them to 'make a match'.

And of S and J:

> T wondered what to say; there was so much pain. From the start, T sensed a desire to reconnect, but, underneath, it also unspoken grief and anger.

Tuning in in this way helps the therapist to access all their intelligences and to focus on the couple and their relationship. (See Chapter 7 for other examples of transference and countertransference).

Taking Note and Notes

All of the above represent issues about which the therapist should take a *mental* note. Despite the cartoon cliché of the therapist listening with pen and notepad in hand, in real life, this is 'not a good look'. The therapist's undivided attention is required to gauge the feeling in the room, and to take account of all that the couple 'says', both verbally and non-verbally.

Written notes are best made after the session when they can provide an invaluable opportunity for the therapist to collect their thoughts and to register, sometimes like a penny dropping, the meaning of what has just been experienced. This adds weight to the suggestion that, where possible, a consultation should involve more than one session, so that the therapist and the couple can feed back their impressions of the first meeting. It models an understanding that a period of reflection is important – that not all impressions are immediately understood, nor do all decisions have to be taken instantly.

CONCLUSION

This chapter has explored the possibilities of first meetings. If nothing else, first meetings prove whether there is a match for continuing couple therapy. If meetings are to continue, there will be a written or verbal agreement setting out the terms. There will also be a shared understanding about the focus of the therapy being on the couple's relationship and the impact on it of their described difficulties; thus the process of assessment will have begun. With everyone's commitment and their engagement with curiosity, the therapy journey can get underway. There is nothing so promising as a good beginning.

LET US ASK OURSELVES ...

*   How easy is it to say to a couple, 'I understand your request, but I cannot offer you the kind of therapy you are seeking'?

CHAPTER SUMMARY

*   This chapter looks at what happens in a couple's first meetings with a therapist and their importance in setting the tone for their work together. Addressing this 'consultation phase', the chapter begins by describing important features established at the outset, such as the 'therapeutic frame', contract making, assessment, and the place of interpretation.

- What questions might a therapist have in making an assessment? Brief case examples illustrate the considerations a therapist makes in assessing whether couple therapy is to be recommended.
- Additional perspectives are offered from other methods of assessment.
- The chapter also discusses note-taking, genograms, and the impact of online therapy on the therapeutic frame.

HAVE YOU READ?

Grier, F. (ed.) (2001). *Brief Encounters with Couples*. London: Karnac.
Lanman, M. (2003). Assessment for Couple Psychoanalytic Psychotherapy. *British Journal of Psychotherapy*, 19(3), 309–323.

REFERENCES

Crawley, J. & Grant, J. (2008). *Couple Therapy*. Basingstoke and New York: Palgrave Macmillan.

Freeman, D.R. (1990). *Couples in Conflict*. Milton Keynes: The Open University Press.

Gottman, J. M. and Silver, N. (1999). *The Seven Principles for Making Marriage Work*. New York: Three Rivers Press.

Grier, F. (ed.) (2001). *Brief Encounters with Couples*. London: Karnac.

McGoldrick, M. & Gerson, R. (1985). *Genograms in Family Assessment*. New York: W.W. Norton & Co.

Morgan, M. (2001). First Contacts: The 'Couple State of Mind' as a Factor in the Containment of Couples Seen for Initial Consultations. In: F. Grier (ed.) *Brief Encounters with Couples* (pp.17–32). London: Karnac.

Scharff, J.S. (2014). Establishing a Therapeutic Relationship in Analytic Couple Therapy. In: D.E. Scharff & J.S. Scharff (eds.) *Psychoanalytic Couple Therapy* (pp.131–147). London: Karnac.

Williams, L. (2022). *Assessment in Couple Therapy: Navigating the 7Cs of Relationships*. London: Routledge.

10

ONGOING MEETINGS AND CHALLENGES IN COUPLE THERAPY

INTRODUCTION: THE ONGOING WORK

This chapter focuses on what might be expected to arise as couple therapy develops. The threesome therapy relationship has its own life cycle which goes through various phases of development. The value of viewing all relationships in terms of their developmental life cycle is discussed at the outset. Five key features of ongoing couple therapy – maintaining the '**therapeutic frame**', confidentiality, depression, the three-way relationship, and '**narcissism**' – are presented with examples of challenges often encountered as therapy progresses, followed by therapists' possible responses.

EXPECT DISRUPTIONS!

After a good enough start to clear the hurdles of consultation, assessment, and contract making, it would be nice to assume that all the couple and their therapist need to do is to apply themselves to an agreed programme. But while a positive beginning is helpful, this does not mean that a route forward will be clearly visible. In fact, to borrow from Shakespeare, the practice of therapy like 'the course of true love,' rarely does 'run smooth'. Although set-backs should be expected as inevitable, they can also be considered as invaluable learning experiences. If we see a couple's challenges to the therapy as the outward signs of troubled inner dynamics in their relationship now getting played out though the therapy, what seem to be set-backs can be used as indicators of what needs to be addressed to resolve their distress. Illustrations of this are given below.

DOI: 10.4324/9781003313403-10

DISRUPTIVE EXTERNAL EVENTS

In 2020, following the COVID-19 lockdown, most therapists were disconcerted by the requirement to move to online meetings. Online therapy, also described in Chapter 9, has existed for several years, and has been preferred by some, especially to bridge distances (Scharff, 2013). Therapists, however, are still evaluating the impact on the therapeutic frame of moving the setting away from more conventional face-to-face meetings. It raises continuing questions about what flexibility or boundaries are truly necessary to safeguard therapy.

THE COUPLE THERAPY LIFE CYCLE

Relationships are dynamic; they live and continually change throughout the lives of the people who are their 'hosts'. Like all living things, without growth, relationships die. Relationships therefore go hand-in-hand with development. Development is either continual, or it is arrested, and growth is the dynamic that drives the relational life cycle, from birth, or beginning, through a maturing process, to death, or ending. If growth is halted in one partner, perhaps by trauma, the couple relationship becomes stuck and unable to progress into its next phase of life.

Thinking about a couple therapeutic relationship, we might have in mind four concurrent life cycles: one for each partner, one for the couple's relationship, and one for the couple therapy. The relationship co-created between couple and therapist can also be seen in developmental terms, passing through beginning, middle, and ending phases. Each phase reflects a couple's particular shared beliefs about relationships.

1. *The initial phase*: like the couple's own relationship, the beginning of therapy may be tentative, with the couple thinking, 'Let's not get our hopes up about this therapy.' Or, it may even be idealistic, when the couple don rose-tinted spectacles, so anxious are they that in this therapist they have found the right match. In the therapist, there is, or should be, a cautious but hopeful acceptance of waiting to discover: 'How are these two people a couple, and can we work together creatively?' To check whether trust, and therefore commitment, is possible,

everyone's reasonable doubts should be aired early on and any unfounded '**idealisations**' set aside.

2. *The middle phase*: therapeutic relationships are unusual in that the last session is anticipated from the first meeting. Potential anxieties for the couple may ensue: 'Will this therapy be long enough and strong enough to see us through?' I suggest that this uncertainty could foster unconscious desires to test the therapy's tensile strength with challenges such as those illustrated in the vignettes below. They are reminiscent of the tests set in so many dependent relationships by behaviour that asks, 'Will you still love me if …?' The therapist should therefore expect challenging behaviour as part of therapy's middle phase. Whether it presents as resistance to keeping to the contract, or the onset of depression in one partner, or the start of an affair, it provides nevertheless a timely reality check. The couple might in effect be saying, 'This therapy was asking too much of us too quickly,' or 'I/we haven't yet been able to speak about something really important …'

Seen in a broader context, there may have been insufficient opportunities in one or both partners' lives to rebel against parents. Throwing down the gauntlet to the therapist may enact, in the '**transference**', hatred felt for parent figures who seemingly still want to control them. Such rejection of therapy is sometimes described as a '**negative therapeutic reaction**'. Just as the couple therapy relationship has its own life cycle, so therapists can also find themselves used in the life cycles of individual partners, standing in for a parent or parents from whom partners or the couple have not yet separated. There is a continuing need to defy that parent, *and* a continuing longing to be accepted.

3. *The ending phase*: the final phase of the therapy relationship life cycle is considered more fully in Chapter 11. Here, however, it is worth remembering that aspects of ending occur throughout therapy and are even implicit from the start. The dependency that therapy offers will ultimately have to be let go. In the meantime, the couple has to learn to tolerate the gaps between sessions and explore whether they can use these intervals to develop their own resources to manage difficulties. A process of disengagement therefore runs parallel with the process of engagement.

FIVE KEY FEATURES OF ONGOING THERAPY AND THEIR CHALLENGES

Five key features of ongoing work are described: maintaining the therapeutic frame, confidentiality, depression, the three-way relationship, and narcissism. Each is highlighted to demonstrate how, as couples respond to therapy, it elicits challenges from them which become important landmarks in the work. Four case examples illustrate the particular characteristics of each feature, although readers will discern a number of shared issues. In particular, narcissism presents so commonly in close relationships that examples of it are found in all four cases illustrated.

MAINTAINING THE THERAPEUTIC FRAME

The 'therapeutic frame', also described in Chapter 5, puts 'protective arms' around couple therapy to safeguard its principal aims. These assert its fundamental beliefs and approach, and it is the therapist's task to hold them in mind so that they can steer the therapy's course. The frame is intended to offer the couple the best chance of achieving their goal, and to provide the therapist with anchorage for work, which can otherwise drift or get blown off course. Keeping a frame in mind, the therapist can try to ensure that the:

- Setting is a safe place so that trust can grow;
- Focus remains on the couple relationship as client;
- Therapeutic relationship is a working one, not a friendship;
- Boundaries and terms agreed in the contract are kept unless renegotiated and never changed arbitrarily;
- Partners' realities are also acknowledged and the pain of the couple's experience is contained.

As explained above, until they trust their therapist's purpose, couples may seek to test these principles.

Challenges to the Therapeutic Frame

Like all clients, couples may find it difficult to work with someone who maintains a different way of thinking and may try, in various ways, to persuade the therapist to 'come over to their side'. It can feel like a tug of war. The therapist's task is to hold on to the centre ground as a safe meeting point.

Example

C and D agreed to meet weekly with **T**. Together for three years, C and D's shared understanding was of having 'an open relationship'. C now suggested, as they both wanted children, it was time to give up other lovers. D was undecided, but agreed to try couple therapy to 'sort it out'. T's assessment was that C and D shared a commitment to being ambivalently attached; couple therapy could only help if it was held within a clearly spelled-out contract.

Initially the three appeared to get on well, and C and D were ready to contract to regular joint attendance. But, over four months, several interruptions caused late arrivals or cancellation, each with a plausible explanation: C's heavy cold; an emergency hospital visit to a relative; D's work interview; a last-minute opportunity to take a 'much needed holiday'. It came to a head when C arrived alone. Twenty minutes later, D texted to say he was 'caught up in heavy traffic'. T, wrong-footed into starting the session, and expecting that, as previously, D was just about to arrive, was then thrown by C's reaction. Clearly feeling stood up, C let slip she was sure D had 'actually gone to have a quickie' with someone else. She added that D thought that, as T (from her wedding rings) was married, she was 'obviously going to be judgemental about our lifestyle'. C asked to meet separately with T to talk about her feelings for D.

T replied that it would be important to arrange to meet *together*, so they could all talk openly about what had happened, and the session ended on that basis. T arranged an early meeting with **S**, her supervisor.

Comments on the Therapist's Response

Hearing from C and D about what they wanted to explore, T recognised their difficulty in committing exclusively to one another, albeit that C saw that this might be preferable if they became parents. T expected this ambivalence to feature in the therapy; agreeing to change meant changing their lifestyle, and probably a sense of their identities. Holding to the therapeutic frame would keep the therapy as a '**secure base**', a security all the more needed because examining reasons for ambivalence about commitment and dependence is never a speedy process. But C and D appeared genuine, likeable, and capable of insight. T was persuaded to continue in good faith.

Predictably, C and D found ways to challenge T's focus on their relationship as client and their contract to joint attendance at pre-arranged times. T felt hampered, however, in challenging them. Seduced by their initial compliance, she feared upsetting the therapy relationship by questioning their commitment. Their working relationship had seemingly become very personalised.

Supervision helped T to consider transference and '**counter-transference**': C and D had turned to T, in their transference to her as a parent, to guide them in their uncertainty about whether to step forward into another (parental) phase of adult life. We might also hypothesise that they shared mixed feelings about whether parents are wholly dependable. C and D therefore enacted between them that T was the needed parent they could do without. Even in C's plea to T to meet her alone, and her 'telling on' D, there were hidden attacks, not only on D, but on T as a couple therapist and on the couple's shared therapy. It certainly raised questions about how the therapy could proceed from there.

In terms of her countertransference, T recognised her maternal feelings towards the couple in wanting to help them. These turned to disappointment and puzzlement as she felt wrong-footed by their attempts to upset their therapy without stating openly that, between them, it was difficult to commit to therapy, let alone to put one another first. It fell to T therefore to be plain-spoken about the need to hold to the frame in order for the therapy to be useful to them.

CONFIDENTIALITY: ETHICAL ISSUES AND THE DOUBLE BIND

Although confidentiality should be regarded as a fundamental principle and part of the therapeutic frame outlined above, it is worthy of highlighting it in its own right. It can emerge in several ways in couple therapy, as shown in the case of C and D, and is always a challenge in terms of sensitive management. Confidentiality helps to build trust, but building any relationship on 'keeping secrets' puts it at risk of collapse. In the case of C and D, the therapist arranged to carry forward the issues raised by C to a session including both partners.

Difficulties most commonly and notably arise when the therapist meets separately with one partner and is told in confidence something that it may be difficult to know how to share.

Example

E and F, heterosexual parents to two daughters, aged five and seven years, have met **T** for couple therapy for eight months. Their relationship is volatile with angry verbal outbursts – reportedly 'non-violent' – where each 'gives as good as they get'. E called T, asking for an extra joint session, saying, 'Something has come up'. On arrival, however, E was alone. Her face looked bruised and swollen. E explained that she and F got into a fight over getting her to return his laptop on which she knew he was looking at porn – she suspected it was images of children. What should she do? If she left him, she had nowhere to go. If she reported him, F would lose his job. He was at work and didn't know she had come to see T. If he did, she was afraid he would 'lose it' and take it out on her and the girls – either that, or 'do something desperate'. E wept, saying that she loved F and was afraid of losing him.

T registered E's state of shock which she also felt. It was important to contain E's fear so that they could both consider what to do. In the first instance, the paramount need was for a place of safety for E and her daughters. T explained the importance that the information E had given her was shared with those who have the full authority to support her. With E's agreement, T called the social work department to refer the family. Then they might decide how to involve F.

Comments on Therapist's Response

E was in a double-bind which she projected onto T. Essentially, it was not T's role to establish whether E's suspicions of F were well-founded, nor whether she and her daughters were at risk, so long as E was able to seek appropriate professional help. In due course, E and F might wish to return to couple therapy, and in the meantime, T was left with the discomfort of holding 'secrets' that F might not be aware that she knew. This couple therapy carries the burden of a confidentiality double-bind; the work cannot progress without openness and honesty, but it would be important not to put E's, the girls', or F's safety in jeopardy. At the same time it is primarily E's responsibility to enable F to know what has been said.

THE BURDEN OF DEPRESSION

The significant impact of depression on couple and family relationships is well recognised by therapists and is the subject of research (Jones & Asen, 2000; Hewison, Clulow, & Drake, 2014). Feeling depressed in response to bereavement, illness, academic or work disappointments, or rejection in relationships may be considered as a normal, healthy way of grieving loss and change, provided that grief then leads to emotional re-adjustment. Being in a couple relationship can provide partners with mutually supportive 'safety nets'.

But sometimes one partner is identified as being more susceptible to deeper depression, perhaps having had a history of episodes. When, from early years, losses are multiple and there has been insufficient loving understanding, depression can recur repeatedly, making sustained engagement in relationships very demanding for both partners.

Example

G and H, a gay couple in their thirties, sought help from **T** to resolve difficulties in 'moving forward'. Together seven years, to their friends they were like 'an old married couple'. H, eldest of three brothers, was outgoing and sociable; G, an only child, was shy and retiring. H, a builder and physically strong, was 'always there' to protect G. Relatively slightly built, G suffered periodically from irritable bowel syndrome and depression. A chef, G preferred his life to be 'in the background'. An opportunity for change came from a possible career promotion for H in another city. He wanted to marry G so they would move as a couple. But G felt overwhelmed by anxiety about H's offer and took to his bed. Both now felt stuck.

Couple therapy over six months gradually shifted their sense of themselves as individuals and as a couple. In T, they saw a father figure who accepted them for themselves. They learned to appreciate that each brought creativity and nurture to their relationship – two gifts that they instinctively knew they would need for survival in a world so often ready to reject them. Rejections hit G bodily and psychologically. H, braved them out. Having been a caring older brother, H enjoyed the strength he felt when comforting G. In fact, ever the upbeat cheerful one, he managed life's repeated knocks by projecting his depression onto G. G, who had never been sure of his father's love, knew that when he was ill, H would love him.

Quietly, however, G despised himself as weak and sickly. Between them, they had created a 'no win' situation.

H's solution to marry and move city was fraught with danger for G, because if it failed they would both lose everything. But the safety afforded by the couple therapy enabled G especially to recognise that he could change the role he had given himself. As he grew stronger, G was less passive and able to recognise his passive aggression in retreating into the role of the continual dependent. He took back the liveliness he had projected into H and came out of his shell.

At first H was delighted, then dismayed. T wondered aloud if H had lost the carer's role on which he had depended. H nodded, but looked crushed, seemingly depressed. After a missed session, T wrote to say that he awaited their return. H returned with G, but was almost speechless with feelings of uselessness and helpless rage: he saw no point in continuing the therapy – where was it going? T was clearly only interested in helping G, and H felt shut out. Getting up abruptly, he walked out. T agreed with G that they should wait for H to come back. As after ten minutes he had not, T promised to write inviting them both to return together at the usual time.

At the next session, H was keen to explain that in walking away from the previous session, he'd had a flashback to an experience fifteen years earlier. In his late teens, he had come out to his father who 'turned on me and cut me dead', told him that he 'would never be anyone', and threw him out of the house. H was depressed at first, lived on the street for a bit, and then by chance got a job on a building site. He 'buried his woes and didn't look back'.

Comments on the Therapist's Response

Early on, T recognised that depression played a powerful part as a third in G and H's relationship. It was a sick role, signalling both a need for dependence and a sense of being unlovable. There were both benefits and costs for G and H that G took this role. If G threw it off, H would have to take back his '**projections**' and allow himself to feel the pain of rejection. Couple therapists note that, not uncommonly, when one partner recovers from depression, the other then succumbs with feelings that they had been silently carrying and managing by vicariously caring for them in their partner. T's task was to wait patiently, to hold the ring, and, in H's terms, 'be there' when needed to acknowledge the pain the couple relationship was bearing. This can be a testing time in therapy as, if a partner gives up hope and walks out, it may be difficult to persuade them to return. When there are crises in therapy, however, the therapist's role has much to do with *being*, rather than reactively doing. When H walked away, T kept the door open, writing to assure them that he looked forward to their next meeting.

THE THREE-WAY RELATIONSHIP

It may be by accident, or by unconscious design, but the three-way relationship created for the purposes of couple therapy has many features that help to bring a couple's difficulties to the fore. At one and the same time, the threesome presents opportunities and inherent difficulties.

Opportunities for the therapist as a third person include:

- Hearing and containing both partners' distress and their shared history;
- Witnessing how partners engage, whether agreeing, disregarding, or quarrelling;

- Presenting an outsider's perceptions of how the couple's relationship appears;
- Modelling how to listen fairly to both parties;
- Modelling toleration of exclusion from a twosome.

Inherent difficulties are:

- Oedipal vulnerabilities in being the outsider with a twosome (see Chapter 7);
- Powerlessness while witnessing verbal and emotionally abusive conflict;
- Resisting side-taking even when provoked by the issues discussed.

An old saying, 'Two's company, three's a crowd', expresses commonly felt inhibitions about interfering in what is going on between two other people. But by seeking out couple therapy, the couple have apparently given authority for the therapist to do just that.

Example

J and K were a same-sex couple in their forties. Together for ten years, they had a four-year-old son, **L**, born to J following IVF. Meeting with **T**, they wanted to address the loneliness both felt in their relationship. Early sessions concentrated on supporting them to manage, at a distance, maternal bereavements in their respective families. Both families were, they said, 'a country away', giving T the impression that, as a lesbian couple, they felt estranged from their cultural backgrounds. After six months, although T felt she engaged with J and K separately, it was hard to address a shared meaning of their loneliness. J engaged T as a maternal figure discussing her experience of perinatal depression. K, as if to a sibling, let T know that, as an organisational consultant, she understood how T saw the world. T felt drawn in to pair with each in turn in their rivalrous bids for her attention; to step back would seem to enact the rejection each feared. After sessions, T began to feel a heavy sense of loss and isolation, as if the gap could not be bridged. She even avoided bringing it to supervision – thinking it would take 'too long to explain'.

Fortuitously, a crisis occurred. K announced a trip away to present a new book. Her solution was that, as they had a 'very poor internet connection at home', J could attend sessions in-person as usual and K would link up with T and J online in T's consulting room. Feeling that this would strain the therapeutic frame, T interpreted to them that this was 'a bridge too far' and wondered aloud why it felt so difficult to explore what connected and disconnected them. It emerged that they had both hoped to be birth mothers, but after K miscarried twice and J had perinatal depression, they felt too wary of 'going through all that again'. T wondered whether their relationship itself had become perinatally depressed (Ludlam, 2014b). Their parents had remained distant and aloof through it all, staying loyal to their cultural rules. Instead, K preoccupied herself in her career, and J 'wrapped herself around' their son, each seemingly excluding the other. The book became K's baby, and J and K stopped seeing themselves as a couple who parented.

T acknowledged the pain of lost hopes, dreams, and children. Especially as L was about to start school, they would all need to think about how J and K could come together to accept and understand one another's shared and respective experiences of loss and isolation.

Comments on the Therapist's Response

Early on, T's allotted role seemed to be that of a supportive witness, with relatively little understanding on the part of the couple that couple therapy involved changes in J and K's relationship. Registering later an expectation of working in a threesome, J and K resisted by each seeking to pair with T. Because she had felt kept at bay, T initially welcomed these overtures, before realising that they trapped her, either into rejecting J and/or K, or into neglecting her proper focus on their couple relationship. She found herself trying to distance herself from them by avoiding thinking about the dilemma even in supervision sessions. When she later consulted **S**, her supervisor, S noted T's avoidance of curiosity, a recognised '**defence**' against unconsciously held fixed beliefs (Morgan & Stokoe, 2014). In her countertransference, might T be responding to aspects of J and K's families' fixed beliefs? S hypothesised that as 'refugees' from their communities, J and K had unwittingly brought with them the 'ghosts' of their families' powerful mindsets, only to find themselves unable to exorcise them without their families' participation.

But it was the stark image created by K's 'solution' of joining online therapy with J and T that freed T into drawing attention to what had been avoided so far. It was as if J and K were finally given permission to explain their sense of being abandoned to a parent who truly wanted to listen and understand. At this point, therapy for their couple relationship could really begin.

NARCISSISM

Last, but by no means least, since so much has been written about it, narcissism presents as a virtual third party in relationships that struggle to grow (Kernberg, 1995; Fisher, 1999; Lackhar, 2004). We note James Fisher writes of 'marriage', although nowadays he might have referred to 'committed couple relationships'. From a couple therapy perspective, Fisher sees narcissism and marriage as opposites; marriage is 'the passion for and dependence on the intimate other' while narcissism is 'an intolerance for the reality, the independent existence of the other' (1999, p.1). Here the otherness, or difference, of the other is crucial. In a mature marriage, the couple achieves a capacity for the mutual recognition and acceptance of difference, alongside their passionate involvement. Regarding narcissism, Fisher notes that despite longing for a relationship, that longing is to find someone who so exactly fits one's own needs that they are not truly 'other' at all. In the narcissist's world, differences are intolerable.

After falling in love with someone who seems so compatible they are like 'a soul mate' or 'a better half', and, as if waking from a dream, it can be a shock to have to accommodate all their differences, and find oneself 'falling out of love' or 'outgrowing one another'. For Fisher, couple therapy might thus be termed 're-marriage', because it entails re-examining the relationship, and potentially re-seeing one's partner and the relationship in their true light, not as we may have assumed them to be. Some couples become stuck because they share a narcissistic commitment to deny their differences which renders any growth impossible.

Reviewing the Above Examples

Unsurprisingly, since their difficulties are prompting them to review their relationships, the four case examples portrayed above all illustrate a number of aspects of narcissistic relating, either as a couple, or in their family relationships.

1. *C and D* (pp.137–139): so much about this couple speaks of non-acceptance of and resistance to difference – the tug of war to hold to the contract, the partners' shared assumption of being equally committed to an open relationship, and that T would readily comply with their needs; i.e., they could have their cake and eat it.

2. *E and F* (pp.139–140): although there does not seem to be narcissistic, coercive control of one partner, the volatility of their relationship suggests difficulties in accepting respective differences, which induces both to act secretively, worryingly in F's case with suspicions of his use of child pornography.

3. *G and H* (pp.140–142): H's need for G to remain dependent as the sick partner held them both in thrall. G also needed to be able to grow. Both suffered from the rigid non-acceptance by family and society of their different sexual orientation. Managing such narcissistic wounds frequently involves depression.

4. *J and K* (pp. 143–145): this couple can be seen as refugees from transgenerational narcissism in the shape of the long-held fixed beliefs systems of their families of origin. Fixed belief systems resist curiosity and outlaw difference. Despite escaping, J and K both unconsciously brought with them the 'ghosts', or deep-seated memories, of their struggles against rejection. They need to lay these ghosts to rest, to be free of their families' narcissistic control in order to share life as a parental couple, rather than live together in loneliness.

CONCLUSION

The above four couple stories illustrate key features of ongoing work that has been interrupted or redirected by dynamics in the couples' relationships. Space precludes the inclusion of more examples, but these are chosen to show how several issues can coincide to affect the course of a therapy.

LET US ASK OURSELVES …

- What couple therapy situations do you feel most challenged by?
- What fixed beliefs are you aware of in yourself and when are they unhelpful to others?

CHAPTER SUMMARY

- This chapter draws attention to resistance and challenges in ongoing therapy which are best regarded as aspects of the couple's relationship, signalling what may otherwise be overlooked
- The therapeutic frame gives therapy the security it requires to be creative, and the three-way relationship allows opportunities to model listening and to contain pain. Nevertheless, three-way relationships have inherent oedipal difficulties which may risk therapists taking sides and keeping secrets.
- Further challenges arise through the need to manage open conflict, or discern and address covert conflict, where partners or children are at risk, and unacknowledged loss and grief may underlie depression in one or both partners.
- An avoidance of curiosity may indicate resistance driven by unconscious fixed beliefs. This is an aspect of narcissism or intolerance of healthy differences, a common feature in couples seeking therapy.

HAVE YOU READ?

Kahr, B. (2018). *How to Flourish as a Psychotherapist.* London: Karnac.

Olds, J. & Schwartz, R.S. (2009). *The Lonely American: Drifting Apart in the Twenty-first Century.* Boston, MA: Beacon Press.

REFERENCES

Fisher, J.V. (1999). *The Uninvited Guest: Emerging from Narcissism Towards Marriage.* London: Karnac.

Hewison, D., Clulow, C., & Drake, H. (2014). *Couple Therapy for Depression.* Oxford: Oxford University Press.

Jones, E. & Asen, E. (2000). *Systemic Couple Therapy and Depression*. London: Karnac.

Kernberg, O.F. (1995). *Love Relations*. New Haven and London: Yale University Press.

Lackhar, J. (2004). *The Narcissistic Borderline Couple*. New York: Brunner Routledge.

Ludlam, M. (2014b). The Perinatally Depressed Couple and the Work of Mourning: A Developmental Imperative. In: K. Cullen, L. Bondi, J. Fewell, E. Francis, & M. Ludlam (eds.) *Making Spaces: Putting Psychoanalytic Thinking to Work* (pp.109–125). London: Karnac.

Morgan, M. & Stokoe, P. (2014). Curiosity. *Couple and Family Psychoanalysis*, 4(1), 42–55.

Olds, J. & Schwartz, R.S. (2009). *The Lonely American: Drifting Apart in the Twenty-first Century*. Boston, MA: Beacon Press.

Scharff, J.S. (2013). *Psychoanalysis Online: Mental Health, Teletherapy, and Training*. London: Karnac.

11

OUTCOMES: ENDINGS AND NEW BEGINNINGS

INTRODUCTION

This chapter addresses the meaning and experience of endings in couple therapy. It begins by arguing that the therapist's approach to endings in relationships is of fundamental importance. This is followed by a discussion of ways in which therapists can facilitate endings so that couples have space to prepare while the inevitability of an ending is kept in mind. Various possible outcomes of therapy are described before considering the question of when to end, and whether, in the aftermath of a relationship, it is ever useful to think about failure, rather than new beginnings.

WHY DOES THE THERAPIST'S APPROACH TO ENDINGS MATTER?

Endings in relationships create milestones in all our lives. This means that therapists should be ready to examine and understand their own beliefs about endings in couple relationships and their desired outcomes of therapy, including:

- What role should a therapist play in the ending of therapy and/or when couples decide to part?
- Crucially, is reconciliation always better than separation or divorce?

DOI: 10.4324/9781003313403-11

Reflecting on these questions, therapists may discover a number of personal motivations for choosing to work in this field. For example, there may be long-held (perhaps unconscious) wishes to address family conflicts in their own lives, such as bringing parents together, keeping the peace, and creating stability. Might these motivations get in the way for the couples who seek help? Perhaps if they are well understood, such motivations can find their proper place. Writing about marriage and divorce, Devorah Baum (2023) notes that two well-known US couple therapists, Esther Perel and Orna Guralnik, are both descended from Holocaust survivors. Transgenerationally, therefore, we might trace back desires to care and repair following trauma.

Ethically speaking, in their practice, therapists should try to maintain an open mind without privileging any particular outcome (Scharff & Bagnini, 2003). This may be more easily said than done; breaking up is always hard, and usually most painful for those who are most vulnerable. Witnessing others' pain and feeling powerless to intervene is extremely stressful. But what matters most is that conflicted couples find the best, or least worst, outcome which they can live with and make work. The pain of relationship breakdown in couples and/or families must be faced and not avoided. Favouring making up over breaking up may (temporarily) serve for therapists to defend against feeling that pain, but accepting and addressing pain may, in fact, be the prime function of the therapy.

These issues relate to how we think about failure – an important aspect of pain which is discussed separately below.

CAN ANOTHER PERSPECTIVE BE FOUND?

In seeking therapy, couples are essentially asking for acknowledgement that they should end their relationship or whether it can be changed. Sometimes their distress is understood in terms of the distance between them – they are either too far apart or too close. Therapy's aim becomes a matter of addressing this, either through helping them to separate, or through re-aligning the relationship so that it feels new or renewed. This chimes with James Fisher's concept of couple therapy leading to a 're-marriage' (Fisher, 1999.

See also Chapter 10). Even after separating, and especially if children are involved, a couple's relationship will continue, albeit more distantly, as one another's 'exes'. Fisher still sees this outcome as a re-marriage, as it is a re-definition of a continuing relationship.

By contrast, other couples, following therapy, sometimes re-take their wedding vows. Hopefully, in that re-commitment they will have found a new, more appropriate, distance between them.

SQUARING UP TO DIVORCE

One of the most important reasons why therapists should closely examine their attitudes to divorce is because it is increasingly likely to be on the agenda of couples who seek therapy. While fewer couples nowadays formally enter a marriage or partnership contract, of those who do, in the UK, almost half (42%) end in divorce. The most common periods for marriage breakups are between one to two years, and between five to eight years. The majority of divorcing couples are in their late forties. There may be many reasons for such statistics, but the influence of cultural norms within a peer group are worth taking into account along with whatever has personally driven each partner and the expectations of the couple. When couples seek help to negotiate ending rather than repairing their relationship, their goal is much more complicated if they have children. (See 'Co-parenting couples' below.)

In her thoughtful chapter entitled 'Divorcing', Baum (2023) sees divorce through several lenses involving novels and films:

- The film: *Marriage Story* (Baumbach, 2019).
- The novel: *Oh William* (Strout, 2021).
- The novel: *Free Love* (Hadley, 2022).

Baum notes the capacity of divorce to free those confined in marriages that are relationally sterile, and, in including Christopher Isherwood's *A Single Man* (1964), which is also a film (Ford, 2009), she observes that profound bereavement on the death of a partner need not foreclose all hope of personal fulfilment.

WHAT IS THE THERAPIST'S ROLE IN MANAGING ENDINGS?

PREPARING THE COUPLE TO LET GO

As set out in Chapter 10, being purposely time-limited, the ending of therapy is anticipated from its beginning. Keeping the '**therapeutic frame**' and the contract in mind, the therapist guides each session to end on time, as well as monitoring the progress of the work towards completion. In shorter, time-limited therapy, its conclusion is more imminent, and this concentrates everyone's minds on what can be done. The fixed date may feel arbitrary, but it is often set to comply with the agency's terms and so the couple and the therapist share the same external controller of the resources. This may also offer some security.

By contrast, in longer-term, time-unlimited therapy, it is the therapist's particular responsibility to assess when the therapy has gone as far as it can. But as well as enabling the therapeutic relationship to be as solid as it can be, the therapist should all along have been preparing the couple eventually to let it go.

UNDERSTANDING THE FEAR OF SEPARATION

Because couple therapy itself involves exploring couples' difficulties about being dependent and about separating, the way the therapist manages endings could be considered more important than how they manage beginnings. From the start, couples may bring the fear of a premature ending, with one partner proposing to leave the other. This makes it all the more significant that a shared understanding about the therapeutic contract embodies planned endings.

Because of its sessional nature, therapy involves continual, planned separations in the gaps between the sessions and over breaks. Observing the couple's responses to these will aid an appreciation of what endings mean for each particular couple. While some endings bring relief – the pain has stopped at last! – other partings are anticipated with such dread that, whether leaving a partner or a therapist, saying farewell is avoided whenever possible. The therapy may end prematurely, with one or both partners abruptly walking out or not attending after breaks, or when an ending is sensed or mooted. It may be that the legacy of earlier separations, in which they were abandoned when growing up, prompts them as adults to be the one who leaves rather than be the one who is left. That way, they retain a sense of control. In those affected by it, separation anxiety may remain a key life-long concern.

Recalling Chapter 2, which touched on the close relationship between separation and dependency, the ability to allow oneself to be dependent requires an ability also to withstand separations. Readers with an interest in attachment theory will here be recalling John Bowlby's *The Making and Breaking of Affectional Bonds* (1979).

The Therapist as a Potential Model

It is, of course, the couple's prerogative to end therapy whenever they so choose. It behoves the therapist, however, to sit with the discomfort of any uncertainty and engage the couple in preparing for ending. If ending therapy coincides with the couple parting, thinking about it inevitably risks being painful. It may, however, lessen some of the pain of grieving separately after final farewells. Some of the most moving writing has come from those whose partners suddenly left them. For example:

- Poems by Sharon Olds, *Stag's Leap* (2012).
- Autobiographical novel by Nora Ephron, *Heartburn* (1983).

Giving Good Notice of Ending

Good notice is the antithesis of walking out, dumping, or abandoning. When the therapist gives notice, it may still be perceived as a rejection, but good notice allows opportunities to grieve, to celebrate, to express disappointments, to consolidate what has been learned, and to say goodbye. In long-term therapy, the length of notice is a matter of negotiation, but an optimal notice period if sessions are weekly notionally might allow a month for every six months of meetings.

Of course, there will be some points in the therapist's life when they themselves will want to take a break, or retire. This is another instance where, if at all possible, it will be very important to prepare couples for this, so as not to leave them 'in the lurch'. If necessary, it may be possible to refer the couple on to work with a colleague, always, of course, after some consultation and preparation.

Nowadays, it has also become common practice, and is even required by some professional bodies, that members identify a colleague whom they name in a 'clinical will.' In the event that the therapist cannot continue working, this person will make arrangements for clients to be informed and for a suitable ongoing referral to be made.

BEING PREPARED TO LET GO

The therapist themselves should of course be ready to let go and not to drag out an ending. It means being able to recognise when the couple is ready to end therapy. It may be that they have become stuck, and need the therapist to help them put into words that the relationship has 'run out of road' and it is time to let it go.

Alternatively, and usually after a sustained period of collaboration to resolve difficulties, there may be recognition that it is time to progress from threesome to twosome work. Ideally, this is when the couple have 'internalised' the therapy relationship as a good **'object'**.

RECOGNISING AN ENDING PHASE

Although it may be thought of as still in working mode, therapy can be considered to be in an ending phase when the couple is feeling a greater sense of autonomy; they are on the road to becoming their own therapist. This is achieved along with what Mary Morgan (2019) describes as a **'couple state of mind'**. Internalising the therapy relationship means that it can live on inside them after meetings have ended, so that the couple can envisage their relationship, as the therapist does, as something between them that is a separate entity in its own right. A couple comes to therapy because they lack such a state of mind, but through sitting with the therapist, they develop it as if by osmosis. The couple in their shared state of mind then becomes something that can support them, as well as something that needs their support. It may be perceived more simply as a shared understanding between a couple, and in effect a dynamic process that needs continual renewal. It can become the arbiter of one another's (and their children's) needs. This will be true both for couples who stay together and for those who separate.

INDICATIONS OF A COUPLE'S READINESS TO END THERAPY

The therapist may also observe notable increases in the following abilities:

- Listening to one another – taking in and tolerating not only the words, but the feelings each expresses.
- Interacting less defensively and allowing separateness and difference in one another.
- Taking time in sessions to be quietly thoughtful.
- Being honest, without needlessly hurting each other.
- Resolving differences and/or making up after a fight.
- Being willing to reflect on the therapy between sessions.
- Resuming enjoying one another, talking together, sex, planning the future.

All of the above will involve partners taking back negative '**projections**'. This involves partners in recognising that particular needs and feelings that they have previously visited on one another should now be more properly owned by themselves, i.e., 'My partner is not controlled by me, and has their own separate being.'

WHAT ARE THERAPY'S POSSIBLE OUTCOMES?

Among the many potential outcomes for couples as they end therapy are:

- Trying another therapist;
- Resolving differences sufficiently to continue their care and repair themselves;
- Progressing to family, individual, and/or sex therapy.

If they decide to separate they may:

- Separate to live apart;
- Seek legal and physical separation in divorce;
- Declare 'conscious uncoupling' (Woodward Thomas, 2015);
- Split up, leaving one partner with the therapist, as the new 'abandoned couple' (Morgan, 2019, p.179) to process what has happened;
- Throw a divorce party.

CO-PARENTING COUPLES

When separating couples have been able to resolve most of their conflict with or without therapy, they are able to work out collaborative agreements to continue as co-parents. The disruption to young children and the cost of running two households have led to the development of arrangements such as 'nesting', i.e., the children remain at home while their parents take it in turns to stay with them.

Sometimes couple therapists continue to be involved in helping separating parents because their unresolved issues can adversely affect co-parenting and their children (Iscoff, 2023; Shmueli, 2023).

Alternatively, couples may seek family mediation to settle parenting differences (Gov. UK., 2023).

SHOULD WE EVER TALK OF 'FAILURE'?

The frequent reference to 'failure' in Chapter 3 suggests how readily it is reached for to explain a lack of strength or ability. Relationship breakdown risks being written off as a sign of personal failure. But whether we consider such a judgement justifiable, the avoidance of addressing feelings of failure in a couple or a therapist cannot wish those feelings away. Our propensity to judge others for their choices in relationships is high, and can be laced with some victim blaming. A phrase from William Congreve's comedy *The Old Bachelor* has crept into common parlance:

> Thus grief still treads upon the heels of pleasure:
> Married in haste, we may repent at leisure.

(Congreve, 1693).

Blame, because of its links with shame and guilt, only increases a sense of failure. Feelings of shame, arising from the fear of being thought unlovable, are experienced very early in life. All human beings thus have an inner relationship with the fear of failure – of falling out of favour with those we love and/or on whom we are dependent. It colours how we feel when others lose relationships or do not meet expectations in relationship.

If we cannot wish or rationalise the sense of failure away, we can, however, find better ways with which to weigh it emotionally so that we can carry it more lightly. Writing about it previously (Ludlam, 2014a), I suggested that couple therapy is predicated on failure, since its task is to address either an impending breakdown, or the aftermath of one that has already occurred. It can, of course, be argued, especially with hindsight, that relationship breakdown is not synonymous with failure. But at the time of a breakdown happening, the feeling of having failed may be trammelled by feelings of grief and guilt as the loss of the relationship is likely to entail a host of other losses.

What of the Therapist's Sense of Failure?

Sometimes the therapy ends in what feels to be a destructively incomplete way, as for example, if the couple 'vote with their feet' by not attending or by walking out, declaring the therapist to be hopeless. In such instances, the therapist can learn from the experience, especially in supervision:

- Is the couple projecting their own fears of failure onto the therapist? Are they leaving because they have themselves written off their own hopes for change?
- Or, as described in Chapter 7, has the therapist been set up to fail by the idealised expectations of the couple?
- Or is there an important message here about the therapist's style of working which merits some critical examination?

For example: has the therapist avoided hearing the pain brought by the couple through intellectualising about their difficulties? '**Intellectualisation**' describes the therapist's '**defence**' used when the couple's feelings become too painful to bear, and rather than responding empathically, '**interpretations**' are offered that are somewhat remote and rational, as if the therapist has not really wanted to engage with them. What the couple really need at such moments is '**containment**', which is discussed more fully in Chapter 7.

In summary, as suggested elsewhere (Ludlam, 2014a), therapists may fall foul as a result of misunderstood factors:

- The assumption that couples seeking therapy really want and believe in the possibility of help.
- The belief that therapists ought to repair all broken relationships, because separation and divorce equal failure.
- Instead of being containing, therapists may easily defend against feelings of powerlessness when witnessing couples' conflict and distress, perhaps by actively intervening, instructing, or intellectualising. Containing provides a different way of 'restoring order' by restoring the capacity to think about what is so disturbing.

SO WHEN CAN THERAPY BE CONSIDERED 'DONE'?

It is sometimes said that at the end of therapy – of whatever kind – the therapist should aim to 'hand back' the problem that the client originally brought to the therapy. Ideally, the 'problem', or the 'sorrow' (see Chapter 3), will have been reviewed and reformulated, so that it can be returned to its owners in a less malign form. Ideally too, what therapy has 'done' to it feels for the couple like a collaborative achievement.

It is also observed that therapy only really starts to work *after* therapy sessions have concluded. In other words, not only does the therapy need to have been internalised and owned by the couple, but they need to be able to put what they have learned into practice without continuing to refer to a therapist. They may continue to consider what the therapist said (or would *now* be saying), but otherwise they have now become their own therapists having made their previous therapist seemingly redundant!

WHAT ENDS WHEN THERAPY ENDS?

This book has reiterated the belief that although relationships change, and indeed they must to survive, they do not end. In everyday terms, relationships continue long after death, or as long as any who are involved are alive. When therapy ends, unless they are moving away or are retiring, the therapist may want to speak of 'leaving the door open' should the couple ever want to return. It is important for the therapist to rehearse privately how to manage a last session, and on what terms to say 'goodbye'.

For example:

- What is said about keeping in touch?
- Many therapists do not encourage physical contact between themselves and their clients. What happens if a client wants to give the therapist a hug?
- Or a present?

The hope with the ending of therapy is that it can be the starting point for continuing learning – in either the couple or the separating partners – as well as for new beginnings. It may lead to further therapy, whether in the individual partners, the couple, or other family members. It is to be hoped that, in some way, therapy can prove to be 'good enough' to be a continuing resource.

LET US ASK OURSELVES ...

- What should be said at a painful, perhaps premature, ending?
- Is there an ideal way to conduct a final session?

CHAPTER SUMMARY

- This chapter has explored the meaning and experience of endings in couple therapy, stressing that the therapist's approach to endings in relationships is of fundamental importance, especially in recognising the significance of divorce.
- The therapist's role in the management of ending processes is discussed, including allowing space to grieve, as well as

assessing when therapy should end. Various different possible outcomes of therapy are considered, followed by discussion of the consideration of when to end.

- The question of how to manage and understand feelings of failure is explored.
- Finally, the chapter addresses what signals the end of therapy and how the last session might play out.

HAVE YOU READ?

'Uncoupled' couple relationships have a long aftermath …

Ahrons, C.R. (1994). *The Good Divorce: Keeping Your Family Together When Your Marriage Comes Apart*. New York: Harper-Collins.

Wallerstein, J.S., Lewis, J.M., & Blakeslee, S. (2000). *The Unexpected Legacy of Divorce: The 25 Year Landmark Study*. New York: HarperCollins.

REFERENCES AND FILMOGRAPHY

Baum, D. (2023). *On Marriage*. London: Hamish Hamilton.

Baumbach, N. (dir.) (2019). *Marriage Story*. Borehamwood, Herts: Heyday Films Ltd.

Bowlby, J. (1979). *The Making and Breaking Of Affectional Bonds*. London: Tavistock Publications.

Congreve, W. (1693). *The Old Bachelor* (repub. 2017). Scotts Valley, CA: Create Space Independent Publishing.

Ephron, N. (1983). *Heartburn*. New York: Alfred A. Knopf.

Fisher, J.V. (1999). *The Uninvited Guest: Emerging from Narcissism Towards Marriage*. London: Karnac.

Ford, T. (dir.) (2009). *A Single Man*. The Weinstein Company.

Gov. UK. (2023). Making Child Arrangements if You Divorce or Separate: Get Help Agreeing. Retrieved 15.03.24 from: https://www.gov.uk/looking-after-children-divorce/mediation.

Hadley, T. (2022). *Free Love*. London: Jonathan Cape.

Iscoff, D. (2023). Co-Parent Therapy and the Parenting Plan as Transitional Phenomena. In: S. Nathans (ed.) *More About Couples on the Couch* (pp.225–241). London: Routledge.

Isherwood, C. (1964). *A Single Man*. New York: Simon and Schuster.

Ludlam, M. (2014a). Failure In Couple Relationships – and In Couple Psychotherapy. In: B. Willock, R. Coleman Curtis, & L.C. Bohm (eds.) *Understanding and Coping with Failure* (pp.65–71). London and New York: Routledge.

Morgan, M. (2019). *A Couple State of Mind*. London and New York: Routledge.

Olds, S. (2012). *Stag's Leap*. London: Jonathan Cape.

Scharff, J.S. & Bagnini, C. (2003). Narcissistic Disorder. In: D.K. Snyder & M.A. Whisman (eds.) *Treating Difficult Couples* (pp.285–307). New York: The Guildford Press.

Shmueli, A. (2023). Discussion of 'Co-Parent Therapy and the Parenting Plan'. In: S. Nathans (ed.) *More About Couples on the Couch* (pp.242–250). London: Routledge.

Strout, E. (2021). *Oh William*. London: Viking.

Woodward Thomas, K. (2015). *Conscious Uncoupling: The Five Steps to Living Happily Even After*. London: Yellow Kite.

12

WHY IS SUPERVISION IMPORTANT FOR COUPLE THERAPY?

INTRODUCTION

This chapter aims to show the importance of supervision in providing couple therapy. As in other talking therapies, supervision offers necessary '**containment**' for the couple therapist, an ethical anchor for the therapy, and thus protection for couples as clients.

Following definitions of terms, including the role of the '**container**', the chapter considers practical issues of cost and frequency. It then explores the benefits of talking with peers about work as therapists, and describes various characteristics of the supervisory relationship: the '**reflection process**', the third position, triangular relationships, and boundaries, before suggesting criteria when in search of good supervision.

DEFINING OUR TERMS

'SUPERVISION' OR 'CONSULTATION'?

The words 'supervision' and 'consultation' are often used interchangeably to describe sources of support, professional development, and where necessary, corrective guidance for the therapist in their working role.

Supervision, literally implying 'overseeing', is sometimes taken to mean:

- Discussion or inspection of work where the supervisee is responsible to the supervisor for the quality of their work,

DOI: 10.4324/9781003313403-12

such as with an employee and employer, or between a student and a tutor.

* In the context of this chapter, the purposeful discussion of counselling or therapeutic work with a colleague.

Consultation, in the context of this book, has two meanings:

* Initial discussion a couple has with a therapist to explore whether couple therapy is right for them (see Chapter 4);
* Discussion a therapist has about their work with a peer – a colleague who is similarly qualified in counselling or psycho-therapy. This may also be referred to as 'peer supervision'. In such a consultation, which literally means 'talking with', the two involved probably think of themselves as equals, and there is no obligation on the consultee to follow the consultant's recommendations or observations.

Most therapists' first experience of supervision is as a trainee. As a newly qualified therapist, this way of discussing their work may feel like a continuation of the tutoring received when training. Because it offers an ongoing learning experience, supervision does represent a continuation of that training, albeit that it now happens with a fellow therapist who will become a peer.

CONTAINER AND CONTAINING

Therapy can be thought of as functioning as a container for trou-bled couples (see Chapters 5 and 7). The idea of containment was first set out by Wilfred Bion (1962) to describe how a mother (or carer) can fully take in their baby's distress while still being able to comfort them. The carer does this by showing that the distress has been heard, and by replying with soothing impres-sions of the pain or upset feelings which 'detoxify' their impact. Bion argued that, like the carer, the therapist can be a container of distress, so that often even feelings that cannot be spoken about can be contained; this enables the client to bear to think about them and learn from them. When it works as it should, supervision can also contain the therapist who has acted as the container of the couple's hurt and distress.

SOME PRACTICAL QUESTIONS OF COST AND FREQUENCY

WHAT DOES IT COST?

Some counselling organisations may provide free supervision to individuals or to groups as part of their contract with their volunteer counsellors. Generally speaking, however, the qualified counsellor or therapist should expect to pay an hourly rate comparable with that paid for individual therapy, but the rate, like the frequency of sessions, is a matter for negotiation between the supervisee and the supervisor.

HOW FREQUENTLY SHOULD SUPERVISION HAPPEN?

Counselling or therapy services each have their own requirements about a required frequency, which is often set as a proportion of the number of client hours worked. For self-employed therapists, frequency of supervision is often stipulated or recommended by the therapist's professional body.

WHY SHOULD THERAPISTS TALK ABOUT THEIR WORK?

IT BENEFITS AND PROTECTS THE CLIENT

Many practitioners feel that once they have qualified, they have 'passed their test' and have proved that they have enough skills to offer clients a good service. In many ways, however, a comparison with a driving test is apposite; passing the driving test alone does not guarantee an immediate qualification to face the challenges of a winding, icy country road or the fast lane of a motorway in a rainstorm. Experience certainly matters, both as a driver and as a therapist.

There are also moral and ethical considerations; we owe it to everyone affected by what we are doing, whether driving or practising therapy, to do it within our capabilities. We need to take time to learn our limitations; to be ever ready for new learning experiences; to recognise that we cannot always predict what we shall meet on the road or in the therapy room; to accept that we have blind spots. My first consultant said to a newly qualified me, both to reassure *and* to forewarn me, 'Don't worry. The first ten years are the worst …!' He was adopting Sigmund Freud's maxim that we should try to learn something from every experience. Essentially, my consultant was agreeing that while such learning can be painful, it is a necessary and continual process.

THE ETHICAL IMPERATIVE

Subjecting their work to others' scrutiny enables therapists to keep up to date with the expectations of professional bodies whose codes of practice give considered responses to the continually changing environment.

Therapists with many years' experience may feel less need of consultation than those who are relatively inexperienced, but talking about one's work is not just good practice for the newly qualified (BACP, 2016). Supervision preserves a place in which to think about a number of different complex ethical principles. For example:

- If we become concerned that someone in the couple's family is at risk of abuse, how should we proceed? It will need careful thinking through.
- We have responsibilities not to exploit troubled couples' vulnerability. There are parallel duties to balance in safeguarding their confidentiality with the requirement to allow our work to be interrogated by colleagues in order to ensure our fitness to practise.

Simply put, whether we regard ourselves as a supervisee or consultee, or indeed as a supervisor or consultant, as practitioners, we owe it to clients, colleagues, and to our profession to continue to think openly about our work. In this way, we can be open to the continuing learning it offers.

IT REWARDS AND PROTECTS THE THERAPIST

Some therapists set up periodic reviews with their clients to assess how the work is going and whether clients' expectations are being met (see also Chapter 11).

Supervision, however, creates a different kind of conversation in a space set apart from therapy sessions with couples. There the therapist can talk in confidence about the experience of being with their couple clients, explore further understanding of the couples' stories, and can get in touch with their own '**transference**' thoughts and feelings, as discussed in Chapter 7. This is especially useful because the experience of being with a couple can be so conflictual and intense, sometimes with each partner rivalrously bidding for support, that it can be hard for therapists to be in touch with their own thoughts. There are strong temptations too to drift unwittingly into trying to offer two people simultaneous individual therapy rather than couple therapy. Regular consultation with a colleague schedules a needed recovery space in which to step back and be aware of what is happening between partners and between oneself and them. Examples of this are given in Chapter 10.

It Empowers the Therapist

Knowing that supervision is going to provide an 'additional ear' enables the therapist to be ready to hear the couple's most distressing feelings, their aggression, their fear, their loss. Without access to a separate, calm thinking space, in which to make sense of it, therapists might be tempted to avoid addressing and feeling this kind of pain with the couple. In this connection, it has been suggested that therapists should be ready to 'catch' their patients' state of mind, like an illness, and to feel the discomfort, so as to empathise truly. This makes for being a good therapist. But the reality is also that feeling the pain of a broken relationship is especially upsetting and a particularly challenging aspect of couple therapy. This is a compelling argument for engaging a supervisor to act as a container and why good therapy is strengthened by good supervision.

HOW TO LOOK FOR GOOD SUPERVISION

Look for Compatibility

When looking for supervision, therapists are best served by working with someone with whom they feel compatible. Most start by seeking someone whom they know to be experienced and respected, and is available to work one-to-one. Some try out several possible supervisory partnerships to find a good match.

Another option is to join a peer group led by a group supervisor – an arrangement that is generally found in counselling services, as well as in training courses.

Compatibility is most often found in someone who shares one's broad approach to couple therapy, and who speaks the same emotional language. Generally, a supervisor's way of listening and thinking aloud reflects their orientation as a practitioner. Do they seem most comfortable as our teachers, correcting our way of working, or reflecting with curiosity with us about what is happening in the work?

COMPLEMENTS OR COMPLIMENTS?

Ideally, therapists can find a supervisor who *complements* them – who sees the gaps in their thinking and practice. It is invaluable to be able to build an honest relationship in which a supervisor can challenge one to take a look at our work from another, perhaps quite different perspective.

Additionally, therapists may also find a supervisor who *compliments* them – who can acknowledge when they are working well. As practitioners we need both.

BEWARE OF COMFORT

Compatibility and trust are essential, but supervisor-supervisee partners should be wary of becoming so comfortable together that they collude to avoid being curious about what is difficult. This may happen quite unconsciously as it can be hard to break up a good working relationship. Who does not enjoy a comfortable rut? But awareness of the risks of collusion has led some professional bodies to recommend changing supervision arrangements every three years. In that way we refresh, if not shake ourselves out of, our comfort zones.

WHAT PREPARATION IS NEEDED?

Generally speaking, time spent preparing for supervision has its own rewards. Writing down thoughts and feelings about a session or sessions in a 'process recording' helps to bring to the surface further realisations about what was being communicated by and between the couple. An example of this in Chapter 7 illustrates the value for therapists of recording immediate thoughts and reactions after a session. It can help to identify what to explore in supervision.

Some sessions may include so much noise, either literally from arguments, or figuratively from disturbing thoughts, or even from deafening silences, that it can seem baffling at the time to hear exactly what is being communicated. An attentive supervisor can listen for and be curious about the possible underlying themes and may help the therapist not only to listen to the couple, but also to themselves. It becomes possible to wonder, 'Why was there such a sense of dread, or hopelessness?' or 'Why was there a sudden urge to get up and leave, or to fall asleep?' In psychoanalytic terms, as also illustrated in Chapter 7, therapists can be supported to be aware of transference and '**countertransference**' and to take them seriously.

In short, supervision gives the therapist a protected opportunity to reflect on, and almost to relive, the experience of being with a couple. This includes making greater sense of feelings stirred up and left behind by couples as they leave. Again, examples are given in Chapters 7 and 10.

Nonetheless, and paradoxically, it can also be invaluable to talk about work that seems to be going well or which is not given much thought because it seems to be unremarkable – its very unremarkable nature may be a clue that it involves issues that the therapist would rather overlook.

LOOKING MORE CLOSELY AT THE SUPERVISORY RELATIONSHIP

THE REFLECTION PROCESS

The 'reflection process', also known as 'mirroring', is a term first coined by Janet Mattinson (1975). Despite sounding the same, this process differs from the 'reflecting' that is done when we think about an issue, or when we feed back to someone what we have heard them say. The 'reflection process' describes a dynamic in which the relationship between a supervisor and a supervisee, and what they feel, do, and say when discussing work with a couple, is unconsciously influenced by what has happened between the supervisee and the couple. For example:

> *T's meeting with A and B*: **T**, a therapist, has arranged an initial meeting with a couple, **A and B**. Although T tries to present herself as open and uncritical, it is clear that A and B feel very vulnerable. They are sensitive to questions about their relationship, parenting, and lifestyle, and say that previous counsellors have been 'hopeless' at helping them.
>
> T brings her concerns about A and B to consider with **S**, a supervisor, whom she knows well. S finds herself becoming uncharacteristically increasingly frustrated and, unusually, even bored by T. S concludes that T has not taken enough trouble to get to know this very distressed couple. She impatiently suggests to T that perhaps she and T should use their remaining time that day to discuss another case, and that T should *either* arrange a further more organised session with A and B, *or* that T should advise A and B that she cannot help them and will refer them on to another therapist.

Bearing in mind issues of transference and countertransference, we might think that what has happened, unusually, between T and S, tells us something important about the dynamics in both sessions – the feelings that were first stirred up and communicated between T and A and B, and later between T and S. The couple's distress, guilt, and worry that no-one would be able to help them had led them to be defensive. Their transference to therapists, based on previous disappointing encounters, was that they would be withholding and unhelpful. Rather than explaining this, they projected their feelings of frustration and hopelessness onto T. T carried these feelings and her reaction to them – her countertransference – with her into her meeting with S. T 'mirrored' them to S, and S, rather than be caught up in the distress of it all, reacted to these feelings, and acted on them by dismissing the feelings, and with them T, and A and B. It was as if S felt that T *and* A and B were inadequate and asking for too much! This dynamic is also known as an '**enactment**'.

When an enactment like this happens, all is not lost if the supervisor and the therapist can stop to take stock. Recognising that something unusual has happened, and wondering what they have been caught up in, may usher in an 'aha' moment. Retrospectively, it is often evident what was happening. Their shared experience mirrors the story which the couple had felt unable to put plainly into words.

Because there is often so much to think about, it is very easy for significant dynamics in an interaction to be overlooked. This makes it important for supervisors themselves to receive supervision, to ensure that in the triangular relationship made between the supervisor, the therapist, and the couple, none of the needs of the three are repeatedly side-lined. A supervisor's supervisor may remind the supervisor to have, and so bolster them in having, a 'helicopter ability' (Hawkins & Shohet, 1989, p.37).

TAKING A STEP BACK: A THIRD POSITION

The ability to take a wider view, sometimes termed a 'helicopter ability', a 'third position', or '**meta position**', is considered invaluable in talking therapies. It describes the act of 'moving in to look closely at an issue and drawing back to take a wider perspective' or of 'standing back from oneself'. Whether as a supervisor or supervisee, the ability to tolerate holding that place, while observing and thinking about what is happening between oneself and others, helps to avoid reacting defensively when differences are becoming apparent. This is clearly useful in couple therapy as well as in supervision. The significance of being able to take and maintain this third position has been emphasised by psychoanalytic thinkers (e.g., Britton, 1989). Patrick Casement (1985) describes a capacity to develop an 'internal supervisor' inside ourselves, with whom we can discuss what is happening *while* we are working.

THE TRIANGLE

Triangles or threesomes create a significant dynamic in most close relationships, as is explored by Francis Grier and colleagues (2005). Examples might be two parents plus child; two partners plus an addiction; two partners plus a lover.

Couple Therapy Triangles

Mattinson (1975) also recognised the significance of triangles for couple therapy and its supervision (Hughes & Olney, 2012).

Figures 12.1 and 12.2 illustrate two basic couple therapy triangles:

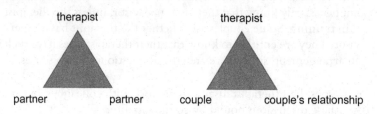

Figure 12.1 Couple therapy triangle 1

Figure 12.2 Couple therapy triangle 2

The Supervisory Triangle

Figure 12.3 shows a simple triangular supervisory relationship. In fact, the supervisory relationship may develop several different triangular relationships. This chapter highlights those that may be most significant in couple therapy, sometimes negatively and sometimes positively.

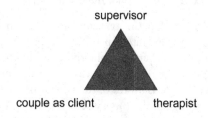

Figure 12.3 Supervision triangle

In the supervisory triangle, as in the couple therapy triangle, each member has the experience of being a 'third', or an outsider, alongside the pairing of the other two. In the supervisory relationship, awareness of outsiderness is invaluable, since it can reflect much of what happens in the therapy room, as well as offering insights into how the couple manages their own twosome relationship with third persons in their lives.

In all the triangles described, each member of the threesome will have the other two in mind, although the client couple will not necessarily know that there is a supervisor, unless the therapist is in training. Some couples ask whether the therapist has a supervisor. They are entitled to know that their therapist does have such an arrangement, since there are ethical questions in two senses:

1. Does their therapist discuss their work with colleagues and are these discussions bound by confidentiality?
2. Does their therapist comply with the ethical code of a professional organisation which requires them to be in regular supervision?

Whether the couple is entitled to know the supervisor's identity is another matter. If such questions are asked, it may be more important to know the reasons for asking, rather than that their apparent curiosity is fully satisfied.

POWER

Power in Triangular Supervisory Relationships

The potential power in the relationship between the supervisor and the therapist is illustrated in Figure 12.3. In that relationship, authority as a practitioner is implicitly given to the supervisor by the therapist, even when the supervisor may be a peer. It is important that the supervisor is aware of the proper use of their power by not taking advantage of the supervisee's relative lack of experience. In the example described above, the therapist, T, was at risk of feeling shamed by the dismissal shown by the supervisor, S. If the supervisor becomes too involved in the difficulties of the client couple, at the expense of what is also happening with the therapist, the therapist may feel abandoned, if not somewhat redundant. After all, the couple A and B remain the clients of T, not of S.

POWER AND COUPLE RELATIONSHIPS

Given the part that power plays in many close relationships, which can lead them to become emotionally and/or physically abusive, it may often be tempting for the therapist to step in as rescuer as in Figure 12.4:

Figure 12.4 Rescuing triangle

The desire to save someone from pain or danger, and to feel effective in situations of powerlessness is very seductive. If the situation with the couple appears perilous, anxiety about it and the temptation to intervene may be so powerful that it is often brought to supervision. If the supervisor catches the anxiety and feels drawn in to be part of the rescue, there is then a risk that they begin to take over, and even to compete with the therapist as the better practitioner, as pictured in Figure 12.5.

Figure 12.5 Rescuing supervisor triangle

It is always salutary to remember that the supervisor's primary focus is on the relationship between the therapist and the couple, not on the relationship between the couple.

BOUNDARIES

WHEN IS SUPPORT UNSUPPORTIVE?

One of the primary words associated with supervision is 'support'. But 'support' for whom, and for what? An important boundary features here:

Supporting the therapist in fulfilling their role has to be separated from any emotional support for the therapist which strays into personal therapy.

The work of the supervisor is to be available to think with the practitioner about their therapeutic work; that in itself is supportive. The supervisor's focus is not on the supervisee's personal emotional needs; attention to what they are feeling is given in order to enable the therapist to understand their feelings about the work, and to use that understanding to provide a better service to the client couple.

Sometimes the therapist may report witnessing something truly shocking, such as an emotionally abusive exchange or an account of an act of physical or sexual violence. Such incidents are very disturbing and distressing. If the therapist is disabled from responding, this has to be talked about. If the therapist feels disabled because what has happened in the therapy brings up disturbing memories from their personal experience, this will also need to be thought about, but in personal therapy, *not* in supervision.

QUESTIONS FOR THE ETHICAL THERAPIST

The ethical therapist will be able to ask themself, 'How do I know whether the difficult situations that I am bringing to supervision have more to do with *me* than with my clients?' A good test might be that if certain situations preoccupy us as therapists, (e.g., we find ourselves repeatedly enacting difficulties, such as responding defensively, or avoiding talking about particular issues), this may suggest that we are looking to our clients to help us to sort out something which may more properly belong elsewhere.

A concern such as this should be first raised in supervision, with questions about whether it should be thought about further in personal therapy.

SUMMARY OF KEY FEATURES
OF GOOD SUPERVISION

A good supervisor …

- *Listens well*: they listen to us listening to ourselves; listen to how we hear what the couple is telling us about their relationship; listen to how we hear how the partners listen to each other; listen to how the relationship between the supervisor and the supervisee might mirror what is happening in the therapy room.
- *Models* how we should learn to consult ourselves. In time, they may become the voice in our ear, an alter ego, which helps us navigate puzzling and challenging experiences. We can learn how to consult ourselves (Casement, 1985), but we should never take our capacities for granted, lest we get into a habit of taking the easy routes, allowing our thought processes to become a closed system circuit.
- *Supports* us in our therapeutic role, but does not stray into offering personal therapy.
- *Challenges* us to recognise blind spots. It is appropriately corrective. Good supervision shows how we might act most professionally in response to demanding situations.
- *Provides* a degree of protection to the client to reduce the risk of harm from poorly practised therapy.
- *Is educative*, showing how we can learn from theoretical concepts as well as what is considered good practice.
- *Is attentive* to our need to review the supervision experience and to give honest feedback about whether needs have been met.
- *Is curious* about the ways in which differences in race, gender, sexuality, and culture may affect the client couple.
- *Is aware* of how what is happening in the world outside the therapy room may be affecting both the client couple and the therapist.

LET US ASK OURSELVES …

- What is more important? That supervisors know about theory or about changes in culture?

CHAPTER SUMMARY

- The chapter seeks to explain the importance of the role of supervision in couple therapy, beginning by defining consultation and supervision.
- It addresses practical questions of frequency and cost, lists the benefits for both client couples and therapists, stressing ethical aspects, and discusses how to look for good supervision.
- The impact of 'the reflection process', of thirds, and triangular relationships is explored and illustrated by diagrams.
- It concludes by discussing boundaries and ethical practice before listing a summary of key pointers to good supervision.

HAVE YOU READ?

This play about the breakdown of a marriage invites us all to be supervisors of the therapy which might be required:

Eliot, T.S. (1950). *The Cocktail Party*. London: Faber & Faber.
Hughes, L. & Pengelly, P. (1997). *Staff Supervision in a Turbulent Environment*. London and Bristol: Jessica Kingsley Publishers.

REFERENCES

Bion, W.R. (1962). *Learning from Experience*. London: Tavistock.
British Association for Counselling and Psychotherapy (BACP) (2016). Good Practice in Action: 043 Supervision Within the Counselling Professions. Retrieved 16.03.2024 from: https://www.bacp.co.uk/events-and-resources/ethics-and-standards/good-practice-in-action/publications/gpia043-supervision-within-the-counselling-professions-ro/.
Britton, R. (1989). The Missing Link: Parental Sexuality in the Oedipus Complex. In: J. Steiner (ed.) *The Oedipus Complex Today*. (pp.83–101). London: Karnac.
Casement, P. (1985). *On Learning from the Patient*, London: Tavistock Publications.
Grier, F. (ed.) (2005). *Oedipus and the Couple*. London: Karnac.
Hawkins, P. & Shohet, R. (1989). *Supervision in the Helping Professions*. Milton Keynes: Open University Press.

Hughes, L. & Olney, F. (2012). Supervision: The Interdependence of Professional Experience and Organisational Accountability. In: A. Balfour, M. Morgan, & C. Vincent (eds.) *How Couple Relationships Shape Our World* (pp.277–295). London: Karnac.

Mattinson, J. (1975). *The Reflection Process in Casework Supervision.* London: Tavistock.

Wheeler, S. & Richards, K. (2007). *The Impact of Clinical Supervision on Counsellors and Therapists, Their Practice and Their Clients: A Systematic Review of the Literature.* London: BACP.

13

HOW CAN I LEARN MORE ABOUT COUPLE THERAPY?

INTRODUCTION

This chapter offers an overview for readers who might want to extend their learning about couple therapy. It should be read in conjunction with Appendix 2, which gives some links to bodies offering training. The chapter strongly advocates joining a taught course in addition to any self-directed learning, because attending and completing a course protects both therapists and clients, and complements what is offered by other learning resources and supportive organisations. The reader is advised about what to look for in a course. As well as theoretical teaching and principles of good practice that tutors model, valuable learning may be acquired from fellow students and personal therapy, and there will also be opportunities to rehearse and demonstrate competence. The emotional rewards associated with such a commitment are emphasised. The chapter concludes with a summary.

THE CONTEXT FOR LEARNING

Learning about human relationships is a natural part of growing up and maturing. Although, as adults, we might hope that we will arrive at a point at which we know enough about relationships, in fact, that learning is a life-long process. Sometimes, however, when we would hope to consider ourselves sufficiently 'grown-up', it can feel as if we are taken back to 'square one', as for example:

DOI: 10.4324/9781003313403-13

- When parenting babies and small children we are reminded of, and re-experience, feelings of bewilderment or anguish which we thought were long passed.
- When losing a loved one through death or irreconcilable differences, we do not know how to begin to grieve or recover.
- As an adult student, it seems as if we know *nothing* about a new field of study, even though it is related to our existing learning.

When learning about therapy, it is especially helpful to confront humbling examples such as these, and to be able to reflect on their particular meaning for each of us. In doing so, it is heartening to recall Sigmund Freud's (1908) maxim that: 'one must try to learn something from every experience.'

Writers of novels and poetry continually strive to explore human relationships and, in particular, the challenges of finding, keeping, and losing love. They thus provide us with a limitless source of material from which to expand our own learning. (See 'Fiction' and 'Poetry' sections in the Bibliography.)

Book groups, study groups, and supervision groups all contribute importantly to ongoing learning and mutual support with peers. Practitioners benefit greatly from seeking out such resources, in what can otherwise be a lonely profession.

THE TRIANGLE OF LEARNING, REGISTRATION, AND PRACTICE

In the UK, the Health and Care Professions Council (HCPC) regulates many professional bodies although, currently, there is no legal requirement that therapists are registered by accredited organisations to practise (see Appendix 2 for links to professional organisations). This lack is regrettable since the criteria for registration safeguard *both* therapist and client. Requirements of therapists include:

- Qualification from an accredited course;
- Professional insurance to practise;
- Commitment to observe a code of practice;
- Evidence of continuing professional development (CPD);

- Endorsement of a fellow qualified member;
- Arrangements for care of clients (a 'clinical will') following death or unplanned retirement.

THE ADDED VALUE OF A FORMAL TAUGHT COURSE

In addition to providing a route to registration, qualification from a course delivered by an accredited training body gives the therapist many benefits, such as:

- Peer group support for learning that is often personally challenging;
- Opportunities to experiment with different techniques and styles of practice;
- A bank of theoretical understanding and resources to draw on throughout one's professional life;
- An understanding of the profession and the environment within which it operates.

WHAT PRE-COURSE QUALIFICATIONS OR REQUIREMENTS ARE NEEDED?

Readers who are contemplating training are encouraged to identify a course that accords with their own approach to human behaviour. (See Chapter 6 and Appendix 2).

Training as a couple counsellor or therapist is usually preceded by a previous qualification in counselling or psychotherapy with individuals. This is sometimes described as a 'foundation course' (see links in Appendix 2 for relevant details on separate courses.) Applicants for couple therapy courses will therefore already have proven their basic aptitudes to work as therapists and be able to demonstrate:

- Ability to show genuine interest in others and awareness of their needs;
- Capacities for listening to others and for self-awareness (listening to oneself);
- Acceptance of others' differences;
- Openness to learning and reflecting on what has been learned.

Infant Observation

Some courses are preceded by courses in 'infant observation', which is now recognised as a standard component of relatively advanced psychodynamic-psychoanalytic trainings because of the valuable insights gained in observing the making of relationships (Hindle & Scott, 2014).

WHAT DO MOST FORMAL COURSES COVER?

As might be expected, courses vary greatly in length and intensity depending on whether they are at Certificate, Diploma, or Doctorate level.

Most syllabi include:

- *Theory and its application to practice*: theoretical teaching will naturally be dictated by the basic concepts of each approach, so that trainees understand the rationale underpinning how they choose to practise.
- *Teaching*: this is usually offered through seminars, group discussion, tutorials, and supervision.
- *Reflective practice*: often modelled in group work, many courses aim to instil in trainees this way of studying their own experiences to enhance the way they work. This is a very useful skill which supports ongoing post-course learning (Wright, 2009).
- *Skills and techniques*: these are tailored to each approach and are often taught in role play. Trainees attending courses teaching relatively longer therapies also work with actual couple clients for periods of up to eighteen months.
- *Supervision*: trainees' work with client couples is discussed and assessed in supervision. This will include presentation of sessions with 'process recordings' in which interactions in a session are detailed to include the therapist's thoughts and feelings and observations of the client's feelings and behaviour.
- *Assessment*: depending on the academic requirements laid down by the body that validates the qualification, some courses require trainees to submit written assignments, case reports, or dissertations. Pre-determined criteria are used to assess a trainee's demonstration of sufficient competencies to qualify and be deemed fit to practise.

- *Personal therapy*: courses that teach psychodynamic-psychoanalytic approaches usually require trainees to receive personal therapy concurrently with the course. This is to ensure that therapists have:
  - Greater familiarity with the processes of psychological change in their clients which therapy may demand;
  - A space in which to reflect on the emotional meaning of a course in couple therapy which may prove (unexpectedly) personally demanding.

WHAT NEXT?

JOINING AND LEARNING FROM PROFESSIONAL PEERS

After qualifying, successful graduates may be eligible to register with a professional association. This will give them the benefits of joining a support network. They will be expected to maintain skills through CPD and to present their work regularly to a supervisor.

FINDING THE LIBERATION OF 'NOT KNOWING'

While it is good to have achieved some competence which can be employed for others' benefit and relief of suffering, it is also liberating to have learned that therapists do not necessarily have to have all the answers. In a letter to his brother, the poet John Keats wrote about the virtues of having:

> Negative Capability, that is, when a man is capable of being in uncertainties, mysteries, doubts, without any irritable reaching after fact and reason
>
> (21 December 1817, Keats, 1899, p.277)

Wilfred Bion (1897–1979), the psychoanalyst, took this up to note the importance of the therapist tolerating not knowing without irritably reaching for rational explanations (1970). In our eagerness to avoid feeling stupid and ineffectual, we can easily replace these feelings with our 'knowing' (see **'intellectualisation'**). Sadly, the road to hell is paved with good intentions. And so it is that we allow our supposed knowledge to get in the way of a couple's discovery of what is most meaningful for *them*.

LET US ASK OURSELVES...

When reviewing an experience that was troubling ask:

- What did I learn about myself as a practitioner?
- What did I learn about myself?

CHAPTER SUMMARY

- The chapter offers an overview for those wanting to extend learning about couple therapy, together with the links given in Appendix 2.
- The value of a formal taught course is emphasised for the benefit and protection of both clients and therapists.
- The chapter suggests what to look for in a course. The particular value of infant observation, reflective practice, process recording, and personal therapy are noted.
- Opportunities for CPD and joining support network groups are noted.

HAVE YOU READ?

Casement, P. (2002). *Learning from Our Mistakes: Beyond Dogma in Psychoanalysis And Psychotherapy*. London: Routledge.

Orbach, S. (2017). *In Therapy: The Unfolding Story*. London: Profile Books.

REFERENCES

Bion, W. (1970). *Attention and Interpretation*. London: Tavistock.

Freud, S. (1908). Letter from Sigmund Freud to C.G. Jung, February 17, 1908. In: W. McGuire (ed.) *The Freud/Jung Letters: The Correspondence Between Sigmund Freud and C.G. Jung*. (pp.119–121). Princeton: Princeton University Press.

Hindle, D. & Scott, A. (2014). Learning from Experience: Developing Observation Skills and Reflective Thinking in Social Work

Practice with Children and Families. In: K. Cullen, L. Bondi, J. Fewell, E. Francis, & M. Ludlam. (eds.) *Making Spaces: Putting Psychoanalytic Thinking to Work*. (pp.75–90). London: Karnac.

Keats, J. (1899). *The Complete Poetical Works and Letters of John Keats*. Cambridge Edition. Cambridge: Houghton, Mifflin and Company.

Wright, J. (2009). Reflective Practice Through a Psychodynamic Lens. In: J. Stedmon & R. Dallos (eds.) *Reflective Practice in Psychotherapy and Counselling* (pp.57–72.). Maidenhead: Open University Press.

APPENDIX 1
Research in Couple Therapy

Several books, as well as articles and review articles, have been based on couple therapy research and/or are useful sources of research material:

Abse, S., Hewison, D., Casey, P., & Meier, R. (2015). *What Works In Relationship Support: An Evidence Review*. London: Tavistock Centre. Retrieved from: https://www.healthymarriageinfo.org/wp-content/uploads/2017/12/20150608EvidenceReview2015 pdf-min.pdf.

Barbato, A. & D'Avanzo, D. (2020). The Findings of a Cochrane Meta-Analysis of Couple Therapy in Adult Depression: Implications for Research and Clinical Practice. *Family Process*, 59(2), 361–375.

Canadian Agency for Drugs and Technologies in Health (CADTH) (2014). *Couples Therapy for Adults Experiencing Relationship Distress: A Review of the Clinical Evidence and Guidelines* [Internet]. Ottawa: Canadian Agency for Drugs and Technologies in Health. Retrieved from: https://www.ncbi.nlm.nih.gov/books/NBK253328/.

Dicks, H. (1967). *Marital Tensions*, London: Tavistock.

Gurman, A.S. & Fraenkel, P. (2002). The History of Couple Therapy: A Millennial Review. *Family Process*, 41(2), 199–259.

Gurman, A.S. (ed.) (2008). *Clinical Handbook of Couple Therapy*. New York and London: The Guilford Press.

Gurman, A.S., Lebow, J.L., & Snyder, D.K. (eds.) (2015). *Clinical Handbook of Couple Therapy* (5th ed.). New York and London: The Guilford Press.

Jones, E. & Asen, E. (2000). *Systemic Couple Therapy and Depression*. London: Karnac.

O'Malley, R., Glenny, R., Poppleton, S., & Timulak, L. (2023). A Qualitative Meta-Analysis Exploring Client-Reported Outcomes of Couple Therapy. *Psychotherapy*, 60(4), 417–430.

Ostertag, P.A. & Regis McNamara, J. (1991). 'Feminization' of Psychology: The Changing Sex Ratio and Its Implications for the Profession. *Psychology of Women Quarterly*, 15(3), 349–369.

Roth, A. & Fonagy, P. (2006). *What Works for Whom? A Critical Review of Psychotherapy Research*. New York: Guilford Press.

Whittaker, K.J., Johnson, S.U., Solbakken, O.A., & Tilden, T., (2022). Treated Together-Changed Together: The Application of Dyadic Analyses to Understand the Reciprocal Nature of Alliances and Couple Satisfaction Over Time. *Journal of Marital Family Therapy* 48(4), 1226–1241.

APPENDIX 2
Organisations Promoting Further Learning

Below are links to some organisations promoting further learning. Readers will readily locate other local resources online.

UK:

PROFESSIONAL BODIES KEEPING REGISTERS OF ACCREDITED COURSES:

- The British Psychoanalytic Council (BPC), www.bpc.org.
- UK Council for Psychotherapy (UKCP), www.psychotherapy. org.uk.
- the British Association for Counselling and Psychotherapy (BACP), www.bacp.co.uk.
- Counselling Directory, www.counselling-directory.org.uk.
- Tavistock Relationships, https://tavistockrelationships.org/ training-courses.
- British Psychotherapy Foundation (bpf), https://www. britishpsychotherapyfoundation.org.uk/education/training/ couple-psychodynamic-psychotherapy/.
- College of Sexual and Relationship Therapists (CoSRT), https://www.cosrt.org.uk/about-cosrt/.
- Marriage Care, https://www.marriagecare.org.uk/.
- OnePlusOne, https://www.oneplusone.org.uk/.
- JCounselling (previously known as Jewish Marriage Counselling), www.jcounselling.org.uk.
- Asian Family Counselling Service, https://asianfamilycoun-selling.org/.
- Relationships Scotland: https://www.relationships-scotland. org.uk/.

SOUTH AFRICA:

- Association of Couple Psychoanalytic Psychotherapists (ACPP), https://acpp.org.za/therapists/.

AUSTRALIA:

- Relationships Australia Victoria, https://www.relationshipsvictoria. org.au/accredited-training/scict/.
- Relational Life Institute, https://relationshipinstitute.com. au/about/.

USA:

- International Psychotherapy Institute, www.theipi.org.
- New York State Education Department CPD (Continuing Professional Development) database, https://www.op.nysed.gov/ professions/marriage-and-family-therapists/continuing-education/providers-list.
- Northern California Society for Psychoanalytic Psychology (NCSPP), https://ncspp.org.

GLOSSARY

Readers may also wish to consult:

Akhtar, S. (2009). *Comprehensive Dictionary of Psychoanalysis.* London: Routledge.

American Psychological Association (n.d.). *Dictionary of Psychology.* Retrieved from: https://dictionary.apa.org.

Feltham, C. & Dryden, W. (2004). *Dictionary of Counselling.* London: Whurr.

Walrond-Skinner, S. (1986). *Dictionary of Psychotherapy.* London: Routledge. (e-Book, 2014. https://doi.org/10.4324/9781315810706).

Coercive control: Formally defined as an act or a pattern of acts of assault, threats, humiliation and intimidation, or other abuse that is used to harm, punish, or frighten a victim; designated a crime in the UK (2015). Arises from pathological narcissism – a fear of loss of control of another, who is not allowed to be different.

Container:
- One who contains, i.e., listens, takes in, and understands another's distress without being overwhelmed, so that thinking about the distress becomes more bearable.
- The therapy – that functions (or contains) as above.
- Containment – the process of containing as above.

Countertransference: This has come to be most usefully thought of as the therapist's experience in response to feelings or states of mind unconsciously communicated by the client (individual or couple). It thus provides important clues to the couple's feelings and experience.

Couple fit: The match between couples' shared unconscious projections resulting in them complementing or becoming complementary to one another.

Couple state of mind/creative couple state of mind: The capacity in a couple to be interested in and talk about their relationship so that they can collaborate creatively to resolve their difficulties.

Defence: A psychological step taken, often unknowingly, to think or behave in a way to protect the sense of self. Defences are important for growth, but may outlive their usefulness.

Enactment: Sometimes called a 'countertransference enactment', this may occur in therapy or supervision when the therapist or supervisor unconsciously responds to feelings stirred up by their countertransference by acting them out.

Idealisation: A defence that enables someone to project only good qualities onto another and to ignore aspects of that other person that do not fit with the ideal. This protects both the one who idealises and the one idealised from bad feelings or disappointments about the other.

Intellectualisation: A defence that enables someone to focus (sometimes rigidly) on rational ways of thinking leading to the exclusion of feelings. The idealisation of reason is used to create a barrier against unmanageable pain or anxiety.

Interpretation: A key technique used in psychodynamic and psychoanalytic therapies with which the therapist feeds back verbally their understanding of the range of impressions and information the couple has presented. The aim is to increase the couple's self-awareness and ability to understand their situation from different perspectives, and thus to enable them to change.

Meta position: Akin to taking a 'third position', or having a 'helicopter ability', this describes the therapist's ability to be both present and metaphorically to 'step back' from what is happening in the therapy session in order to be able to view it from another perspective.

Narcissism: A preference for, and preoccupation with, one's own needs to the exclusion of others. In extreme cases, this presents as an inability to accept that others can have different thoughts and needs, and leads to having rigid or fixed beliefs.

Negative therapeutic reaction: A dynamic sometimes occurring in the process of therapy after there has been some progress, when the client/couple reacts by resisting further work and by disengaging emotionally and/or physically from the therapy. It may, however, prove possible to use this as a helpful learning experience.

Object: A caricatured representation (good or bad) of a significant relationship internalised during psychological development that unconsciously influences how and what relationships are made, unless or until it is reviewed.

Object relations theory/therapy: Psychoanalytic theory (and therapies derived from it) which focusses on relationships with 'objects' rather than Freud's focus on the function of instinctual drives.

Problem formulation: The summing up of the therapist's assessment of a difficulty and the steps needed to remedy it.

Projection: The unconscious attribution of an aspect of oneself (bad or good) onto someone else. It is projected because it is unwanted and therefore not owned.

Projective identification: Frequently occurring in close relationships, this happens when a person unconsciously responds to another's projected feelings or judgement about them, by identifying with them and behaving accordingly.

Reflection process: Also known as 'mirroring'. A process or experience in supervision when the relationship between the supervisor and the therapist mirrors what was happening between the therapist and the couple (client) who are being considered.

Repression: A key feature of object relations theory describing the process of the 'splitting off' of painful, perhaps traumatic, experiences, and putting them out of reach of recall, into the unconscious. At significant moments – perhaps after a trauma or major change – there is a return of what has been repressed, i.e., the honeymoon is over.

Secure base: A key concept in attachment theory, this describes a source of security to which we turn in times of stress and danger, and on which further development and creativity can be built.

Therapeutic frame: This describes the boundaries within which there has been an agreement between the therapist and the client – the ground rules – which enable the therapy to take place.

Transference: The client (partners or couple) unconsciously displaces or transfers onto the therapist aspects of relationships that were significant earlier in life, relating to the therapist as if they were, e.g., a mother, father, or sibling.

Triangulation: A term often, but not exclusively, used in systems theory to describe the way in which two people (notably a couple) avoid addressing a difficulty between them by drawing in a third person, e.g., a child, a parent-in-law, a therapist.

BIBLIOGRAPHY

NON-FICTION:

Abse, S. (2022). *Tell Me the Truth About Love: 13 Tales from the Therapist's Couch.* London: Ebury Press.

Abse, S., Hewison, D., Casey, P., & Meier, R. (2015). *What Works In Relationship Support: An Evidence Review.* London: Tavistock Centre. Retrieved from: https://www.healthymarriageinfo.org/wp-content/uploads/2017/12/20150608EvidenceReview2015pdf-min.pdf.

Ahrons, C.R. (1994). *The Good Divorce: Keeping Your Family Together When Your Marriage Comes Apart.* New York: HarperCollins.

American Psychological Association (APA) (2022). Demographics of U.S. Psychology Workforce. Retrieved from: https://www.apa.org/workforce/data-tools/demographics.

Balfour, A. (2021). A Brief History of Tavistock Relationships. In: M. Waddell & S. Kraemer (eds.) *The Tavistock Century: 2020 Vision* (pp.175–182). Bicester: Phoenix.

Balfour, A., Morgan, M., & Vincent, C. (2012). *How Couple Relationships Shape Our World.* London: Karnac.

Balint, E. (1968). Unconscious Communication Between Husband and Wife. In: S. Ruszczynski (ed.) (1993). *Psychotherapy with Couples.* (pp.30–43). London: Karnac.

Barbato, A. & D'Avanzo, D. (2020). The Findings of a Cochrane Meta-Analysis of Couple Therapy in Adult Depression: Implications for Research and Clinical Practice. *Family Process*, 59(2), 361–375.

Bateman, A. & Fonagy, P. (2012). *Handbook of Mentalizing in Mental Health Practice.* New York: American Psychiatric Publishing.

Bates, L., Hoeger, K., Stoneman, M-.J., & Whitaker, A. (2021). *Domestic Homicides and Suspected Victim Suicides during the Covid-19 Pandemic 2020–2021.* London: Home Office.

Retrieved from: https://assets.publishing.service.gov.uk/media/6124ef66d3bf7f63a90687ac/Domestic_homicides_and_suspected_victim_suicides_during_the_Covid-19_Pandemic_2020-2021.pdf.

Baum, D. (2023). *On Marriage*. London: Hamish Hamilton.

Bion, W.R. (1962). *Learning from Experience*. London: Tavistock.

Bion, W.R. (1970). *Attention and Interpretation*. London: Tavistock.

Bowlby, J. (1979). *The Making and Breaking of Affectional Bonds*. London: Tavistock Publications.

Bowlby, J. (1988). *A Secure Base: Clinical Applications of Attachment Theory*. London: Routledge.

British Association for Counselling and Psychotherapy (BACP) (2016). Good Practice in Action: 043 Supervision Within the Counselling Professions. Retrieved from: https://www.bacp.co.uk/events-and-resources/ethics-and-standards/good-practice-in-action/publications/gpia043-supervision-within-the-counselling-professions-ro/.

British Psychoanalytic Council (BPC) (2023). Bibliography on Gender, Sexuality and Relationship Diversity. Retrieved from: www.bpc.org.uk/?s=GSRD+Bibliography.

Britton, R. (1989). The Missing Link: Parental Sexuality in the Oedipus Complex. In: J. Steiner (ed.) *The Oedipus Complex Today* (pp.83–101). London: Karnac.

Bubenzer, D.L. & West, J.D. (1993). *Counselling Couples*. London: Sage.

Calman, M. (1980). *But It's My Turn To Leave You*. London: Mandarin.

Campbell, C. (2023). *Sex Therapy: The Basics*. London: Routledge.

Charura, D. & Lago, C. (eds.) (2021). *Black Identities and White Therapies: Race, Respect and Diversity*. Monmouth: PCCS Books.

Casement, P. (1985). *On Learning from the Patient*. London: Tavistock Publications.

Casement, P. (2002). *Learning from Our Mistakes: Beyond Dogma in Psychoanalysis and Psychotherapy*. London: Routledge.

Chew-Helbig, N. (2023). How does Psychotherapy Work? General Systems Theory and Synchronization. *The Psychotherapist*. Retrieved from: https://nikhelbig.at/how-does-psychotherapy-work-general-systems-theory-and-synchronization/.

Christensen, A., Doss, B.D., & Jacobson, N.S. (2014). *Reconcilable Differences: Rebuild Your Relationship by Rediscovering the Partner You Love – Without Losing Yourself* (2nd ed.). New York: The Guilford Press.

Clulow, C. (1985). *Marital Therapy: An Inside View.* Aberdeen: Aberdeen University Press.

Clulow, C. (ed.) (2001a). *Adult Attachment and Couple Psychotherapy.* London: Brunner Routledge.

Clulow, C. (2001b). Attachment, Narcissism, and the Violent Couple. In: *Adult Attachment and Couple Psychotherapy* (pp.133–151). London: Brunner Routledge.

Cowan, C.P. & Cowan, C.A. (2000). *When Partners Become Parents: The Big Life Change for Couples.* Mahwah, NJ: Lawrence Erlbaum.

Crawley, J. & Grant, J. (2008). *Couple Therapy.* Basingstoke and New York: Palgrave Macmillan.

Crowe, M. & Ridley, J. (2000). *Therapy with Couples: A Behavioural-Systems Approach to Couple Relationship and Sexual Problems* (2nd ed.). Oxford: Blackwell.

Cullington, D. (2008). *Breaking Up Blues: A Guide to Survival And Growth.* London: Routledge.

Davids, M.F. (2011). *Internal Racism.* London: Bloomsbury.

Dicks, H.V. (1967). *Marital Tensions.* London: Tavistock.

Egan, G. (1994). *The Skilled Helper.* New York: Brooks Cole Publishing Company.

Finkel, E. (2017). *The All-or-Nothing Marriage.* Boston: E.P. Dutton.

Fisher, J.V. (1999). *The Uninvited Guest: Emerging from Narcissism Towards Marriage.* London: Karnac.

Fonagy, P. (1989). On Tolerating Mental States: Theory of Mind in Borderline Patients. *Bull. Anna Freud Centre,* 12, 91–115.

Fonagy, P. (1999). The Male Perpetrator: The Role of Trauma and Failures of Mentalization in Aggression Against Women: An Attachment Perspective. *The 6th John Bowlby Memorial Lecture,* London: The Centre for Attachment-based Psychoanalytic Psychotherapy.

Freeman, D.R. (1990). *Couples in Conflict.* Milton Keynes: The Open University Press.

Freud, S. (1908). Letter from Sigmund Freud to C.G. Jung, February 17, 1908. In: W. McGuire (ed.) *The Freud/Jung Letters:*

The Correspondence Between Sigmund Freud and C.G. Jung. (pp.119–121). Princeton: Princeton University Press.

Freud, S. (1930a). *Civilisation and its Discontents* (standard edition, 21, pp.1–273). London: Hogarth.

Galdiolo, S., Culot, S., Delannoy, P., Mauroy, A., Laforgue, F., & Gaugue, J. (2022). Harmful Stress-Related Couple Processes during the COVID-19 Pandemic and Lockdown. *Frontiers in Psychology*, 13.

Gottman, J. M. & Silver, N. (1999). *The Seven Principles for Making Marriage Work*. New York: Three Rivers Press.

Gov. UK. (2023). Making Child Arrangements if You Divorce or Separate: Get Help Agreeing. Retrieved from: https://www. gov.uk/looking-after-children-divorce/mediation.

Greenberg, L. & Johnson, S.M. (1988). *Emotionally Focussed Therapy for Couples*. New York: The Guilford Press.

Grier, F. (ed.) (2001). *Brief Encounters with Couples*. London: Karnac.

Grier, F. (2005). *Oedipus and the Couple*. London: Karnac.

Gurman, A.S. (ed.) (2008). *Clinical Handbook of Couple Therapy*. New York and London: The Guilford Press.

Gurman, A.S. & Fraenkel, P. (2002). The History of Couple Therapy: A Millennial Review. *Family Process*, 41(2), 199–259.

Gurman, A.S., Lebow, J.L., & Snyder, D.K. (eds.) (2015). *Clinical Handbook of Couple Therapy* (5th ed.). New York and London: The Guilford Press.

Harrison, J. (2020). *Five Arguments All Couples (Need To) Have*. London: Profile Books.

Harway, M. (2005). *Handbook of Couples Therapy*. Hoboken, NJ: Wiley.

Hawkins, P. & Shohet, R. (1989). *Supervision in the Helping Professions*. Milton Keynes: Open University Press.

Hewison, D. (2014). Projection, Introjection, Intrusive Identification, Adhesive Identification. In: D.E. Scharff & J.S. Scharff (eds.) *Psychoanalytic Couple Therapy: Foundations of Theory and Practice* (pp.158–169). London: Karnac.

Hewison, D., Clulow, C., & Drake, H. (2014). *Couple Therapy for Depression*. Oxford: Oxford University Press.

Hindle, D. & Scott, A. (2014). Learning from Experience: Developing Observation Skills and Reflective Thinking in

Social Work Practice with Children and Families. In: K. Cullen, L. Bondi, J. Fewell, E. Francis, & M. Ludlam (eds.) *Making Spaces: Putting Psychoanalytic Thinking to Work*. (pp.75–90). London: Karnac.

Hughes, L. & Olney, F. (2012). Supervision: The Interdependence of Professional Experience and Organisational Accountability. In: A. Balfour, M. Morgan, & C. Vincent (eds.) *How Couple Relationships Shape Our World* (pp.277–295). London: Karnac.

Hughes, L. & Pengelly, P. (1997). *Staff Supervision in a Turbulent Environment*. London and Bristol: Jessica Kingsley Publishers.

Iscoff, D. (2023). Co-parent Therapy And The Parenting Plan as Transitional Phenomena. In: S. Nathans (ed.) *More About Couples on the Couch* (pp.225–241). London: Routledge.

Jacobs, M. (2010). *Psychodynamic Counselling in Action*. Los Angeles and London: Sage.

Jervis, S. (2011). *Relocation, Gender, and Emotion: A Psycho-Social Perspective on the Experiences of Military Wives*. London: Karnac.

Johnson, S.M. (1996). *Emotionally Focussed Marital Therapy*. New York: Brunner Mazel.

Johnson, S. M. (2008). *Hold Me Tight: Your Guide to the Most Successful Approach to Building Loving Relationships*. London: Little, Brown & Co.

Johnson, S.M. (2019.) *The Practice of Emotionally Focused Couple Therapy: Creating Connection* (3rd ed.). London: Routledge.

Jones, E. & Asen, E. (2000). *Systemic Couple Therapy and Depression*. London: Karnac.

Jung, C.G. (1928). Marriage as a Psychological Relationship. In: *Contributions to Analytical Psychology* (pp.189–203). London: Kegan Paul, Trench, Trubner & Co.

Kahr, B. (2018). *How to Flourish as a Psychotherapist*. London: Karnac.

Kernberg, O.F. (1995). *Love Relations*. New Haven and London: Yale University Press.

Knee, C. Raymond, (1998). Implicit Theories of Relationships: Assessment and Prediction of Romantic Relationship Initiation. *Journal of Personality and Social Psychology*, 74(2), 360–370.

Kohut, H. (1984). *How Does Analysis Cure?* Chicago: University of Chicago Press.

Lackhar, J. (2004). *The Narcissistic Borderline Couple*. New York: Brunner Routledge.

Lago, C. & Smith, B. (eds.) (2010). *Anti-Discriminatory Practice in Counselling and Psychotherapy*. London: Sage.

Lanman, M. (2003). Assessment for Couple Psychoanalytic Psychotherapy. *British Journal of Psychotherapy*, 19(3), 309–323.

Lennon, R. (2023). *Wedded Wife: A Feminist History of Marriage*. London: Aurum Press.

Lewin, K. (1952). *Field Theory in Social Work*. London: Tavistock.

Ludgate, J. & Grubr, T. (2018). *The CBT Couples Toolbox*. Eau Claire, WI: PESI Publishing.

Ludlam, M. (2014a). Failure in Couple Relationships – and in Couple Psychotherapy. In: B. Willock, R. Coleman Curtis, & L.C. Bohm (eds.) *Understanding and Coping with Failure* (pp.65–71). London and New York: Routledge.

Ludlam, M. (2014b). The Perinatally Depressed Couple and the Work of Mourning: A Developmental Imperative. In: K. Cullen, L. Bondi, J. Fewell, E. Francis, & M. Ludlam (eds.) *Making Spaces: Putting Psychoanalytic Thinking to Work* (pp.109–125). London: Karnac.

Ludlam, M. & Nyberg, V. (eds.) (2007). *Couple Attachments*. London: Karnac.

McCann, D. (2022). *Same-Sex Couples and Other Identities: Psychoanalytic Perspectives*. London: Routledge.

McGoldrick, M. & Gerson, R. (1985). *Genograms in Family Assessment*. New York: W.W. Norton & Co.

Malcolm, J. (2007). *Two Lives: Gertrude and Alice*. New Haven and London: Yale University Press.

Mattinson, J. (1975). *The Reflection Process in Casework Supervision*. London: Tavistock

Maxwell, J. A., Muise, J., MacDonald, G., Day, L.C., Rosen, N.O., & Impett, E.A. (2016). How Implicit Theories of Sexuality Shape Sexual and Relationship Well-Being. *Journal of Personality and Social Psychology*, 112(2), 238–279.

Mitchell, S.A. (2003). *Can Love Last? The Fate Of Romance Over Time*. New York: Norton.

Morgan, M. (2001). First Contacts: The 'Couple State Of Mind' as a Factor in the Containment of Couples Seen for Initial Consultations. In: F. Grier (ed.) *Brief Encounters with Couples* (pp.17–32). London: Karnac.

Morgan, M. (2005). On Being Able to be a Couple: The Importance of a 'Creative Couple' in Psychic Life. In: F. Grier (ed.) *Oedipus and the Couple* (pp.9–30). London: Karnac.

Morgan, M. (2019). *A Couple State of Mind*. London and New York: Routledge.

Morgan, M. & Stokoe, P. (2014). Curiosity. *Couple and Family Psychoanalysis*, 4(1), 42–55.

Nathans, S. (2023). *More About Couples on the Couch*. London: Routledge.

Nathans, S. & Schaefer, M. (2017). *Couples on the Couch*. London: Routledge.

National Records of Scotland (2013). Population Estimates by Marital Status for Scotland. Retrieved from: https://www.data.gov.uk/dataset/c04cc034-9978-4de8-9116-12ebd3497462/population-estimates-by-marital-status-for-scotland.

Novakovic, A. & Reid, M. (eds.) (2018). *Couple Stories*. Abingdon: Routledge.

Nyberg, V. (2021). Review of *Marriage Story*. *Couple and Family Psychoanalysis*, 11(1), 94–98.

Nyberg, V. & Hertzmann, L. (2019). Mentalization-based couple therapy. In: A. Balfour, C. Clulow, & K. Thompson. (eds.) *Engaging Couples* (pp.130–143). Abingdon: Routledge.

O'Malley, R., Glenny, R., Poppleton, S., & Timulak, L. (2023). A Qualitative Meta-Analysis Exploring Client-Reported Outcomes of Couple Therapy. *Psychotherapy*, 60(4), 417–430.

O'Shaughnessy, R., Berry, K., Dallos, R., & Bateson, K. (2023). *Attachment Theory: The Basics*. New York and London: Routledge.

Office for National Statistics (2021). *Population Estimates by Marital Status and Living Arrangements, England and Wales*. Retrieved from: https://www.ons.gov.uk/peoplepopulationandcommunity/populationandmigration/populationestimates/bulletins/populationestimatesbymaritalstatusandlivingarrangements/2020.

Office for National Statistics, Census (2021). *Divorces in England and Wales*. Retrieved from: https://www.ons.gov.uk/peoplepopulationandcommunity/birthsdeathsandmarriages/divorce/bulletins/divorcesinenglandandwales/2022.

Olds, J. & Schwartz, R.S. (2009). *The Lonely American: Drifting Apart in the Twenty-first Century*. Boston, MA: Beacon Press.

Orbach, S. (2017). *In Therapy: The Unfolding Story.* London: Profile Books.

Ostertag, P.A. & McNamara, J.R. (1991). 'Feminization' of Psychology: The Changing Sex Ratio and Its Implications for the Profession. *Psychology of Women Quarterly*, 15(3), 349–369.

Perel, E. (2006). *Mating In Captivity: Reconciling the Erotic and the Domestic.* New York: HarperCollins.

Perel, E. (2017). *The State of Affairs: Rethinking Infidelity.* New York: Harper.

Pickering, J. (2008). *Being in Love: Therapeutic Pathways through Psychological Obstacles to Love.* London: Routledge.

Pincus, L. (ed.) (1960). *Marriage: Studies in Emotional Conflict and Growth.* London: Institute of Marital Studies.

Roiphe, K. (2008). *Uncommon Arrangements: Seven Marriages in Literary London 1910–1939.* London: Virago Press.

Rose, P. (1983). *Parallel Lives: Five Victorian Marriages.* London: Chatto & Windus.

Roth, A. & Fonagy, P. (2006). *What Works for Whom? A Critical Review of Psychotherapy Research.* New York: The Guilford Press.

Ruszczynski, S. (1993). *Psychotherapy with Couples.* London: Karnac.

Sayers, J. (2021). *Sigmund Freud: The Basics.* London: Routledge.

Scharff, D.E. (2016). The Contribution of Enrique Pichon-Rivière. *Couple and Family Psychoanalysis*, 6(2), 153–158.

Scharff, J.S. (2013). *Psychoanalysis Online: Mental Health, Teletherapy, and Training.* London: Karnac.

Scharff, J.S. (2014). Establishing a Therapeutic Relationship in Analytic Couple Therapy. In: D.E. Scharff & J.S. Scharff (eds.) *Psychoanalytic Couple Therapy* (pp.131–147). London: Karnac.

Scharff, J.S. & Bagnini, C. (2003). Narcissistic Disorder. In: D.K. Snyder & M.A. Whisman (eds.) *Treating Difficult Couples* (pp.285–307). New York: The Guilford Press.

Scharff, D.E. & Scharff, J.S. (2011). *The Interpersonal Unconscious.* Lanham, MD: Jason Aronson.

Scharff, D.E. & Scharff, J.S. (2014). *Psychoanalytic Couple Therapy: Foundations of Theory and Practice.* London: Karnac.

Shmueli, A. (2023). Discussion of 'Co-Parent Therapy and the Parenting Plan'. In: S. Nathans (ed.) *More About Couples on the Couch* (pp.242–250). London: Routledge.

Strober, M. & Davisson, A. (2023). *Money and Love: An Intelligent Roadmap for Life's Biggest Decisions.* San Francisco: Harper One.

Thompson, K. (2015). Review of *her*. *Couple and Family Psychoanalysis*, 5(1), 1107–1111.

Usher, K., Bhullar, N., Durkin, J., Gyamfi, N., & Jackson, D. (2020). Family Violence And COVID-19: Increased Vulnerability and Reduced Options for Support. *International Journal of Mental Health Nursing*, 29(4), 549–552.

Usher, S.F. (2008). *What Is This Thing Called Love?* London: Routledge.

Wallerstein, J.S. & Kelly, J.B. (2004). *Surviving the Breakup*. New York: Basic Books.

Wallerstein, J.S., Lewis, J.M., & Blakeslee, S. (2000). *The Unexpected Legacy of Divorce: The 25 Year Landmark Study*. New York: HarperCollins.

Wheeler, S. & Richards, K. (2007). *The Impact of Clinical Supervision on Counsellors and Therapists, Their Practice and Their Clients: A Systematic Review of the Literature*. London: BACP.

Whittaker, K.J., Johnson, S.U., Solbakken, O.A., & Tilden, T. (2022). Treated Together-Changed Together: The Application of Dyadic Analyses to Understand the Reciprocal Nature of Alliances and Couple Satisfaction Over Time. *Journal of Marital Family Therapy*, 48(4), 1226–1241.

Williams, L. (2022). *Assessment in Couple Therapy: Navigating the 7Cs of Relationships*. London: Routledge.

Winn, R. (2018). *The Salt Path*. London: Penguin.

Winnicott, D.W. (1971). The Use of an Object. In: *Playing and Reality* (pp.86–94). London: Tavistock.

Woodward Thomas, K. (2015). *Conscious Uncoupling: The Five Steps To Living Happily Even After*. London: Yellow Kite.

Wright, J. (2009). Reflective Practice Through a Psychodynamic Lens. In: J. Stedmon & R. Dallos (eds.) *Reflective Practice in Psychotherapy and Counselling* (pp.57–72.). Maidenhead: Open University Press.

Zeitner, R. (2012). *Self Within Marriage: The Foundation for Lasting Relationships*. New York: Routledge.

ADDITIONAL BOOKS ON SKILLS:

Bobes, T. & Rothman, B. (2002). *Doing Couple Therapy: Integrating Theory with Practice*. New York: Norton.

Brent, B.A. & Furrow, J.L. (2013). *Emotionally Focused Couple Therapy for Dummies*. Ontario, Canada: J. Wiley & Sons.

Culley, S. (1990). *Integrative Counselling Skills*, London: Sage.

Howard, S. (2017). *Skills In Psychodynamic Counselling and Psychotherapy* (2nd ed.). London: Sage.

Payne, M. (2010). *Couple Counselling: A Practical Guide*. London: Sage.

Sperry, L. & Peluso, P. (2019). *Couple Therapy, Theory, and Effective Practice* (3rd ed.). London: Routledge.

Treadway, D.C. (2020). *Treating Couples Well: A Practical Guide to Collaborative Couple Therapy*. London: Routledge.

FILMS / TV:

Baumbach, N. (dir.) (2019). *Marriage Story*. Borehamwood, Herts: Heyday Films Ltd.

Bergman, I. (dir.) (1973). *Scenes from a Marriage*. Sverige Radio.

Ford, T. (dir.) (2009). *A Single Man*. The Weinstein Company.

Haneke, M. (dir.) (2012). *Amour*. Les films du losange.

Jonze, S. (dir.) (2013). *her*. Warner Bros.

Kapur, S. (dir.) (2023). *What's Love Got to Do with It?* StudioCanal UK.

Kriegman, J. (dir.) (2019–2023). *Couples Therapy* [TV show]. Showtime / BBC TV.

Logan, J. (dir.) (1958). *South Pacific*. 20th Century Studios.

McGuigan, P. (dir.) (2017). *Film Stars Don't Die in Liverpool*. Sony Pictures Classics.

Nichols, M. (dir.) (1966). *Who's Afraid of Virginia Woolf?* Warner Bros.

FICTION:

Albee, E. (1962). *Who's Afraid of Virginia Woolf?* New York: Atheneum Books.

Barnes, J. (2011). *The Sense of an Ending*. London: Jonathan Cape.

Barnes, J. (2014). *Levels of Life*. London: Vintage.

Byatt, A.S. (1990). *Possession*. London: Chatto & Windus.

Congreve, W. (1693). *The Old Bachelor*. (repub. 2017). Scotts Valley, CA: Create Space Independent Publishing.

Ebershoff, D. (2000). *The Danish Girl*. New York: Viking Press.

Eliot, G. (1870–1871). *Middlemarch*. London: William Blackwood and Sons.

Eliot, T.S. (1950). *The Cocktail Party*. London: Faber & Faber.

Ephron, N. (1983). *Heartburn*. New York: Alfred A. Knopf.

Greene, G. (1951). *The End of the Affair*. London: Heinemann.

Greer, A.S. (2008). *The Story of a Marriage*. London: Faber & Faber.

Hadley, T. (2022). *Free Love*. London: Jonathan Cape.

Hartley, L.P. (1953). *The Go-Between*. London: Hamish Hamilton.

Hooper, C. (2013). *The Engagement*. London: Jonathan Cape.

Isherwood, C. (1964). *A Single Man*. New York: Simon and Schuster.

Lawrence, D.H. (1915). *The Rainbow*. London: Methuen & Co.

McEwan, I. (1992). *Black Dogs*. London: Jonathan Cape.

McEwan, I. (1997). *The Comfort of Strangers*. London: Vintage.

McEwan, I. (2007). *On Chesil Beach*. London: Jonathan Cape.

McEwan, I. (2014). *The Children Act*. London: Vintage.

Nicholls, D. (2014). *Us*. London: Hodder & Stoughton.

O' Farrell, M. (2022). *The Marriage Portrait*. London: Vintage Books.

Raisin, R. (2022). *A Hunger*. London: Jonathan Cape.

Shakespeare, W. *The Winter's Tale*. Retrieved from: https://www.folger.edu/explore/shakespeares-works/the-winters-tale/read/.

Strout, E. (2021). *Oh William*. London: Viking.

Tolstoy, L. (1878). *Anna Karenina* (repub. 1965). New York: Random House. Updike, J. (1960). *Rabbit, Run*. London: Andre Deutsch.

White, P. (1955). *The Tree of Man* (repub. 1994). London: Vintage Classics.

Yates, R. (1961). *Revolutionary Road*. Boston: Little, Brown.

Yglesias, R. (2009). *A Happy Marriage*. New York: Scribner.

POETRY:

Burns, R. (1785). To a Louse. In: (2011). *The Complete Poems and Songs of Robert Burns*. Glasgow: Waverley Books Ltd.

Donne, J. (1624). *Meditation 17: Devotions Upon Emergent Occasions*. (repub. 2015). Cambridge: Cambridge University Press.

Keats, J. (1899). *The Complete Poetical Works and Letters of John Keats*. Cambridge Edition. Cambridge: Houghton, Mifflin & Company.

Kipling, R. (2020). *The Best of Rudyard Kipling*. Redditch, Worcestershire: Read Books Ltd.

Larkin, P. (1960). Talking in Bed. In: (1964). *The Whitsun Weddings*. London: Faber & Faber.

Marlowe, C. (1600). The Passionate Shepherd to His Love. In: R. Clay (1862). *Poets of the Elizabethan Age* (pp.21–22). London: Sampson Lowe & Co.

Olds, S. (2012). *Stag's Leap*. London: Jonathan Cape.

Yeats, W.B. (1920). The Second Coming. In: *The Collected Poems of W.B. Yeats*. Ware: Wordsworth Editions Ltd.

JOURNALS:

Couple and Family Psychoanalysis (from 2011). London: Phoenix Publishing.

Couple and Family Psychology: Research and Practice (from 2011). Washington, DC: American Psychological Association Div. 43.

Family Process (from 1962). Hoboken, NJ: Wiley-Blackwell.

International Review of Couple and Family Psychoanalysis (from 2007). Published online in English / French / Spanish: https://aipcf. net/revue/.

Journal of Couple and Relationship Therapy (from 2002). New York: Taylor and Francis.

Journal of Marital and Family Therapy (from 1975). Hoboken, NJ: Wiley.

INDEX

Printed in the United States
by Baker & Taylor Publisher Services